Helion & Company Limited
Unit 8 Amherst Business Centre
Budbrooke Road
Warwick
CV34 5WE
England
Tel. 01926 499 619
Email: info@helion.co.uk
Website: www.helion.co.uk
Twitter: @helionbooks
Visit our blog http://blog.helion.co.uk/

Published by Helion & Company 2024
Designed and typeset by Farr out Publications, Wokingham, Berkshire
Cover designed by Paul Hewitt, Battlefield Design (www.battlefield-design.co.uk)

ISBN 978-1-804514-67-2

British Library Cataloguing-in-Publication Data
A catalogue record for this book is available from the British Library

We always welcome receiving book proposals from prospective authors.

CONTENTS

ABBREVIATIONS

AAA *Alianza Anticomunista Argentina*/Argentine Anti-Communist Alliance (Triple A)
ARA *Armada de la República Argentina*/Argentine Navy Ship
BAM *Base Aérea Militar*/Military Air Base
CGT *Confederación General del Trabajo*/General Confederation of Labour
EGP *Ejército Guerrillero del Pueblo*/People's Guerrilla Army
ERP *Ejército Revolucionario del Pueblo*/People's Revolutionary Army
FAL *Frente Argentino de Liberación* or *Fuerzas Argentinas de Liberación*/Argentine Liberation Front or Argentine Liberation Forces
FAP *Fuerzas Armadas Peronistas*/Peronist Armed Forces
FAR *Fuerzas Armadas Revolucionarias*/Revolutionary Armed Forces
FMA *Fábrica Militar de Aviones*/Military Aircraft Factory
NCO Non-Commissioned Officer
PFA *Policía Federal Argentina*/Argentine Federal Police
PRT *Partido Revolucionario de los Trabajadores*/Workers' Revolutionary Party

ACKNOWLEDGEMENTS

The author wishes to express his deep gratitude to Argentine aviation historians Esteban Raczynski, Argentine Air Force NCO (Ret.) Walter Marcelo Bentancor, Walter Vladimiro Cettolo and Atilio Marino, the *Archivo General de la Nación* and the *Dirección de Estudios Históricos de la Fuerza Aérea Argentina* for the invaluable data and photographs for this volume.

INTRODUCTION

International Marxist terrorism was able to win the sympathy of many university students, Catholic movements and intellectuals in Argentina in the 1960s and 1970s, using terms such as 'dependency', 'imperialism', 'subjugation', 'colonialism' and 'dictatorship'. In fact, many of these young people had been catechists linked to the Movement of Priests for the Third World, but instead of taking the peaceful path of Christian preaching, they chose the bloody path of armed subversion. Marxism-Leninism managed to penetrate the minds of socially well-off young people, convincing them that the only valid alternative to military dictatorships and Yankee imperialism was violent struggle. This is how they recruited hundreds of young people who later saw their lives and dreams cut short by a useless fight against a well-armed and highly professional Argentine Army.

By 1975, the situation with the guerrillas became untenable, as they had infiltrated factories, workers' unions, schools, universities and even the Federal Police and the armed forces, looking for supporters who would later provide key information for the various attacks they carried out, causing hundreds of innocent victims. In the mid-1970s, these guerrilla organisations had some 5,000 organised, armed, equipped and trained combatants and some 20,000 peripheral militants who were part of the logistics chain or were simply sympathisers. Other sources suggest higher numbers being involved, some 30,000 combatants and 150,000 people, again including members of the logistics chain and supporters. Even so, those numbers represented barely 0.5 percent of the population, and the vast majority of the country were against them. The subversives did have the support of the Soviet Union, Cuba and communist countries of Eastern Europe, and also of left-wing organisations in France, Italy, Germany, the Netherlands, Belgium and Sweden.

Although the first groups of guerrillas began to form after the overthrow of Argentine president General Juan Domingo Perón in 1955 – most of them encouraged by the former president himself in the late 1950s and early 1960s – the main insurgent groups would only appear towards the end of the 1960s. They aimed to prepare the ground for Perón to return to the country and regain the presidency. Perón himself called them the 'Wonderful Youth', but he had created a monster that he could not handle in his later years.

All these groups were inspired by the successful Cuban revolution of 1959 led by Fidel Castro, together with the Argentine freedom fighter Ernesto Guevara, known as 'Che', and unrealistically thought that they could seize power and turn Argentina into a socialist homeland in the best Cuban style. But Argentina was not Cuba, and the Argentine armed forces, although having deep differences and internal conflicts, were still very powerful, well-armed and well-trained, their members being highly motivated to defend the political model in force at the time.

A few examples of the many children killed by subversive organisations in Argentina. (CELTYV Archives)

The subversive bands' objective was to produce chaos in the country, infiltrating the mass Peronist support, destroying institutions and inspiring violence against the state. To achieve their aims, the guerrilla groups resorted to the most despicable acts, including the kidnapping for ransom of politicians, police and military officers, diplomats, national or foreign businessmen, or their relatives. They also took part in hijackings, the seizing of prisons to free their fellow terrorists and launching bomb attacks on the homes of politicians and military officers, factories backed by foreign capital, police stations and military bases. Other tools in their armoury included the assassination of politicians, police and military officers, even including former president General Aramburu.

Every act they perpetrated had the objective of creating chaos in the country to prepare for the return of Juan Domingo Perón as the nation's leader. When the military governments gave way to free elections, with the Peronist candidate Héctor Cámpora winning in 1973, guerrilla activity did not decrease but rather increased significantly. Cámpora belonged to the Peronist left and was greatly influenced by his two *Montonero* sons, so key government positions were held by *Montoneros* (see Chapter 1). This cost him a severe reprimand from the Peronist leader, and when General Perón assumed the presidency again in 1973 he declared all the insurgent groups illegal and launched a military campaign against them. But there was also the Peronist right wing in the General Confederation of Labour (*Confederación General del Trabajo*/CGT) and later the so-called Triple A (Argentine Anti-Communist Alliance/*Alianza Anticomunista Argentina*) led by José López Rega, which would be responsible for avenging those murders and kidnappings of trade unionists by Marxist groups, especially between 1973 and 1975.

General Perón did not live long after becoming president again, and it was his wife Isabel, the vice-president, who, upon assuming the presidency, had to face the serious problem of the guerrillas. Although her government ordered Operation Independence (*Operativo Independencia*), she would not live to see its completion either, which would occur under another military government, the one led by Lieutenant General Videla, towards the end of the 1970s.

This volume covers the long period that runs from the overthrow of the government of General Perón in 1955 until 1974, the year prior to the launch of *Operativo Independencia*, including all the subversive groups that appeared during that time, their main leaders and actions. Of all these groups, only two were protagonists of the most violent crimes in the mid-1970s in Argentina, the People's Revolutionary Army (*Ejército Revolucionario del Pueblo*/ERP) and the *Montoneros*.

This work also examines the organisation of all Argentine government security forces during this period, including the Air Force, the Navy, the Army, the National Gendarmerie and the Argentine Federal Police.

The text of this volume is based on the archives of the Argentine Army, Navy, Air Force and Federal Police, although guerrilla sources were also consulted to cross-reference 'official' data, much of which is unreliable.

1
SUBVERSIVE GROUPS IN ARGENTINA, 1955–1974

In 1955 and 1956, armed Peronist groups began a series of regular attacks, mainly actions of sabotage, the planting of explosives, protests on public roads and boycotts. It was an incipient attempt at armed struggle, the main purpose of which was the return of Perón. The insurgents would end up being appeased after the executions that took place in June 1956, but would re-emerge – with greater vigour – after the rise to power of Arturo Frondizi in 1958.

Resistencia Peronista (1955–1958)

The Peronist Resistance started immediately after the Liberating Revolution (*Revolución Libertadora*) in 1955. Its militants mainly used Molotov cocktails to attack whichever suitable target they could find to let the government know of its existence. In addition, they trained a large number of youngsters in the use of firearms and explosives. In 1956, the attacks gained greater magnitude. On 26 February, a group of saboteurs blew up the powder depot of the Military Communications Materials Factory located in Migueletes, north of Greater Buenos Aires. In the following days, explosives

Members of the Peronist Resistance of Rosario (mainly workers) in a meeting towards the end of the 1950s. The emblem of the movement is on the right (the central shape is red outlined in black, on a white background). (Open Source)

One of the most notorious leaders of the Peronist left, John William Cooke. (Open Source)

were found on the train tracks of the Retiro-Tigre branch, for which four people were convicted. In Rosario, meanwhile, workers from a coffee bottling plant were detained when they were preparing homemade explosives, and in Río Segundo, Córdoba, numerous people – mostly workers – were arrested and accused of violent acts, almost all of them committed between 12 January and 27 February of that year.

The most serious of these events took place in the second half of 1956, when anonymous hands placed an explosive device in the legal office of Dr José Aguirre Cámara, a member of the Advisory Board that advised the government. In Mendoza, another 75 people were arrested for distributing flyers in the street; and in Buenos Aires, agitators stoned the windows of the newspapers *La Prensa* and *La Nación*, with abusive slogans painted on the walls of the capital and other major cities.

All these actions took the government – headed by Lieutenant General Pedro Eugenio Aramburu and Admiral Isaac Francisco Rojas – by surprise, leading to a series of raids and arrests that had as a corollary an increase in repression and the implementation of greater security measures. There then followed further clandestine meetings, the distribution of leaflets on public roads, strikes and boycotts, with many people arrested under accusation of performing violent acts. Immediately after the failed civil-military coup of General Juan José Valle in 1956 (the first uprising against the military government of President Aramburu, with Valle being captured and executed), the attacks and demonstrations faded away until Dr Frondizi came to power in 1958.

From that moment on, labour and student protests became frequent, acts of sabotage occurred again and fresh explosive attacks took place, which is why, on 14 November 1958, the new president put into effect the CONINTES Plan (Internal Commotion of the State). He secretly signed Decree No. 9880/58, which would only be made public in 1962, with Law No. 15,293 on the Suppression of Terrorist Activities, approved on 21 July, after the modification of the Penal Code. It is estimated that between 1955 and 1958, the Peronist Resistance detonated some 7,000 explosive devices all over the country. One of the most prominent leaders of this movement was the lawyer John William Cooke (1919–1968), especially during

Members of the *Tacuara* Nationalist Movement, dressed in Nazi style. Only the swastika was missing, although it was used in their attacks against the Argentine Jewish community. (Open Source)

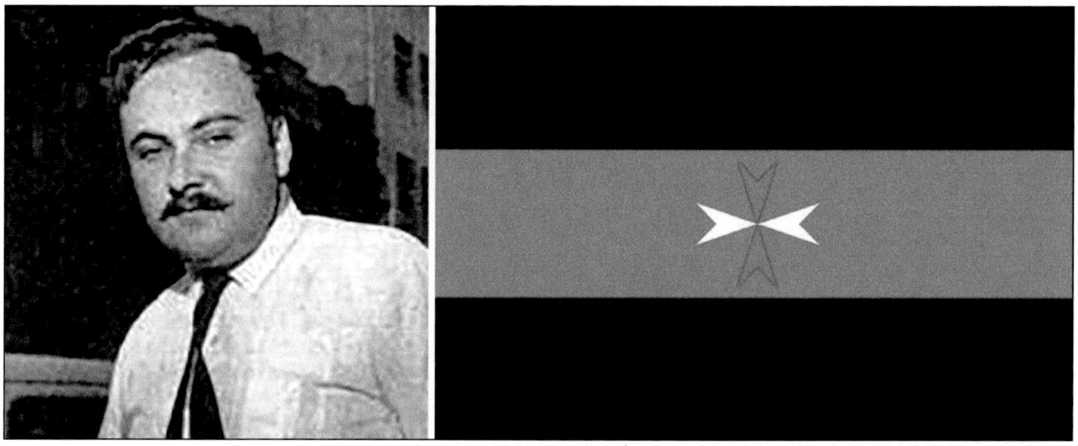

On the left, 'Joe' Baxter, one of the main leaders of *Tacuara*. On the right, the *Tacuara* flag (top and bottom bands in black, central band in red, cross verticals in blue with horozontals in white). (Open Source)

the military regimes of the Liberating Revolution and the Argentine Revolution.

It was in this context that a first guerrilla movement arose in the province of Tucumán, something that had not happened in Argentina since the distant times of Martín Miguel de Güemes and his *gauchos*[1] during the early nineteenth century War of Independence, triggering a little-known war of particular characteristics.

Movimiento Nacionalista Tacuara (MNT) (1957–1966)

Tacuara (a *Guaraní* language word meaning 'bamboo') was an extreme right-wing organisation that emerged after the fall of Perón in 1955, which up to mid-1963 was behind 50 incidents and at least three terrorist attacks. They had Catholic priest Julio Meinvielle as their spiritual guide, with French philosopher Jacques de Mahieu as their inspiration and adviser. Both de Mahieu and Father Meinvielle instilled nationalist ideals in the young students who joined their ranks by the dozens. Although the organisation had been operating since the fall of Peronism, it became official only two years later when it began to recruit young people from the high bourgeoisie and the Buenos Aires aristocracy *en masse*, preferably members of the Nationalist Union of High School Students (UNES). The group inculcated in its members a Catholic, nationalist and above all fascist ideal, which developed in them strong anti-communism and anti-Semitism. Its militants wore very short hair and a grey armband with the Maltese cross on their right arm, and made the Roman salute to identify each other and at demonstrations.

The organisation's main leaders were José Baxter, known as Joe, Catholic priest Alberto Ignacio Ezcurra Uriburu and the activists Eduardo Rosa and Oscar Denovi. The first manifestations of extreme violence occurred in 1962, when they established links with the Arab League, which promoted the war against Zionism and the state of Israel around the world. *Tacuara* joined the league and began attacks against the Jewish community in Argentina, one of the largest in the Americas. Thus was launched a violent campaign that had its peak on 27 April 1964, during a convention held at the Buenos Aires Theatre, where anti-Semitic flyers were handed out and walls were painted with the slogan 'Nasser and Perón, one heart'.

The movement showed signs of cracking in 1964 when its members began to disagree with Perón, causing its first fissure. The supporters of Father Meinvielle opposed adopting the Justicialist line (the largest branch within Peronism) and, led by Roberto de Estrada and Roberto Etchenique, withdrew to found the Nationalist Restoration Guard (GNR), which had an authoritarian Rosas and Falangist tendency (they were led by José Antonio Primo de Rivera). De Mahieu's group maintained its fascist position and the faction of the ever-present Dardo Cabo later broke away from him by founding the New Argentina Movement (MNA), after a pronounced shift to the left. Baxter went much further, abjuring ultra-rightist preaching and shaping, along with José Luis Nell, the *Tacuara* Nationalist Movement (MNT), with a marked Marxist inclination, a line from which, years later, the Peronist Armed Forces (*Fuerzas Armadas Peronistas*/FAP) and even the *Montoneros* would emerge.

Tacuara's first actions took place in 1956, with clashes during demonstrations, political acts and student protests, especially against leftist elements. During the Frondizi government, they defended the position of free education, engaging in fierce combat against those who supported secularism, and in 1959 they desecrated the Jewish cemetery of *La Tablada*, destroying tombstones and painting swastikas. The following year, its leadership focused its actions on the kidnapping of the Nazi war criminal and then Argentine citizen Adolf Eichmann by Israel's *Mossad*, accusing the Argentine government of being complicit and inept. On 17 August 1960, students from the *Domingo Faustino Sarmiento* National School,

SS-Obersturmbannführer Adolf Eichmann in 1942 (left), posing as Ricardo Klement in Argentina in the 1950s (centre) and at his trial in Israel in which he received the death sentence in 1961 (right). (Open Source)

Two Argentine journalists in front of a wall where a swastika was painted by members of *Tacuara* in the early 1960s. (Open Source)

the security forces claimed that he was wounded by a stone thrown by a group of Jews who were preparing to defend a community college threatened by *Tacuara*, a version of events that seemed to confirm an apology made by *La Luz*, a magazine distributed among the Jewish community.

The anti-Semitic violence in Argentina was denounced by the World Jewish Council held in New York, before the United Nations, where it also warned about the intentions of the American Nazi leader George Lincoln Rockwell to establish contact with the *Tacuara* leadership, and the solidarity and support of the Arab peoples for the campaign that the movement carried out against international Zionism

who were active in their ranks, attacked fellow Jews, and on the same day shot and injured Edgardo Trilnik, aged just 15, when a celebration was held in memory of General San Martín, the hero of the War of Independence. Bombs were also placed and detonated in synagogues, schools and Jewish entities, marches were organised and leaflets were distributed supporting fascism, Nazism and Peronism.

Eichmann's kidnapping and subsequent execution in 1962 was followed by a wave of attacks on Jewish synagogues, cemeteries, schools and businesses. This led the Argentine Israelite Mutual Association (*Asociación Mutual Israelita Argentina*/AMIA) and the Delegation of Argentine Israelite Associations (*Delegación de Asociaciones Israelitas Argentinas*/DAIA) to organise a day of protest for 28 June of that year, which was joined by militants from almost all political parties, as well as students and intellectuals from different backgrounds.

The situation seemed to have gotten out of hand when on Tuesday, 21 June 1962, members of *Tacuara* kidnapped Graciela Narcisa Sirota, a 19-year-old Jewish student of Economic Sciences, while she was waiting for a bus to go to college. A vehicle containing three individuals stopped next to the bus stop, and its occupants forced her to get in, taking her to an uninhabited building and subjecting her to torture, burning different parts of her body, beating her and cursing her. The barbarity came to an end when the girl was thrown unconscious into a quiet street in the city, after a swastika had been engraved on her right breast. According to statements made by the victim at the time of filing her complaint, her captors told her that her ordeal was a message to the authorities regarding the Eichmann case.

At that time, it was said that *Tacuara* maintained close ties with elements of the armed forces and security organisations, which provided them with weapons and protection, as well as with well-known Nazis and fascists living in Argentina in the time of Perón. Proof of this collusion was the attitude of the police when investigating the cases of Graciela Sirota and Raúl Alterman, a young man from La Paternal, with the suspects denying the charges and assuring that on both occasions the complainants themselves 'had inflicted their injuries'. In the case of Sub-Inspector Angelici, in Buenos Aires.

The events seemed to shake the apathy of the Argentine government, which through Decree No. 3134/63, signed on 29 April by President José María Guido and the Minister of the Interior, General Enrique Rauch, labelled *Tacuara* and the Nationalist Restoration Guard as illegal groups and went on to hunt down their leaderships. Nevertheless, on the rainy morning of 29 August 1963, a *Tacuara* command group from the MNT – comprising José Luis Nell, Carlos Arbelos, Horacio Rossi, Jorge Caffatti, Ricardo Viera, Rubén Rodríguez and Mario Duahy – attacked the Banking Polyclinic located at 2100 Gaona Avenue, in front of Plaza Irlanda, in the so-called *Operación Rosaura*, taking 14 million pesos after killing two employees and seriously injuring four others.

In March 1964, members of *Tacuara* shot dead Raúl Alterman, a young Jew with a well-known leftist militancy, as he was leaving his home on Azcuénaga Street. The organisation sent a harsh letter to his parents, stating, among other things, that 'No one kills randomly; your son was killed because he was a communist Jewish dog. All Jewish dogs and exploiters must be withdrawn to their native Judea. What are they doing in Argentina?'[2]

Such an act of folly ended up unleashing the indignation of broad sectors of society, although gaining the approval of others, and thus, during the government of Dr Arturo Illia, the persecution against neo-fascist groups intensified. Many of their leaders went to prison and others were silenced, waiting for 'better times' to revive their cause. That, and the constant divisions produced by the deranged ideological turns manifested by some of its leaders – Baxter and Cabo, for example, turned to the extreme left, denying their fascist, Catholic and anti-Semitic preaching – ended up undermining *Tacuara*'s structure and taking it to dissolution. Its members dispersed and, a few years later, became part of the far-left and far-right terrorist groups that devastated Argentina in the 1970s.

The *Uturuncos* (1959–1960)

Uturunco is a *Quechua* language word meaning 'Puma', 'Tiger' or 'Jaguar'. In 1959, the first rural guerrilla organisation with a Peronist tendency appeared in Argentina. Its leader was Manuel Enrique

A group of *Uturuncos* in 1959 in a Tucumán forest (left). The emblem of the *Uturuncos* (La Mañana Neuquén) (red star with white 'U') (right). (Open Source)

Mena, known as *Comandante Uturunco*. This guerrilla group acted in the area adjacent to the Cochuna River, some 120km south of Tucumán. The subversive group was officially called the Peronist Liberation Movement (MPL), but its members were known as the *Uturuncos*. Many of its members had belonged to the Nationalistic Liberating Alliance (*Alianza Libertadora Nacionalista*/ALN), a faction of revolutionary Peronism led by John W. Cooke, and were also members of the Socialist Party of the National Revolution. Initially they only had 20 members, who settled in the hills of Cochuna and El Calao in the province of Tucumán on 21 September of that year. They recruited some 150 other people from the area for their initial logistics chain. The group's members collected weapons, ammunition, explosives, food, money and communication equipment, and their first actions included exploration of the area, the installation of camps and military training.

Towards the end of 1959, they began their first subversive actions, storming small police stations – mainly to steal arms and ammunition – and kidnapping travellers in the area to obtain money. They had very few combatants at this time and were poorly trained and armed. Indeed, it was soon revealed that these subversives were not yet ready to fight. On 24 December 1959, some of them were rounded up by police forces, who ultimately arrested three of their members, including Franco Luppi, known as *El Tano*. The rest of the *Uturuncos* troops were divided into two sections, the first under the command of Mena and the other under Félix Serravalle.

As in any left-leaning group, the disparity of positions on political-military issues divided its members in a fruitless internal struggle. There were acts of indiscipline and desertions, a logistical system that did not work and disorganisation in relation to the objectives of their attacks. The low night temperatures, scarcity of food and activities of the police undermined the morale of the weakest, leading to more desertions taking place. This produced the eventual disintegration of the group, with most of its leaders being captured by the security forces in early 1960. Manuel E. Mena and Juan Carlos Díaz were sentenced to seven years in prison, Félix Serravalle (known as *Comandante Puma*) to four-and-a-half years, and José Luis Rojas, known as *Zupay*, and Santiago Molina (*El Mejicano*) to three-and-a-half years each.

Once the rural guerrillas were defeated, the *Uturuncos* increased its actions in the urban area. On 15 February 1960, its militants blew up the Shell-Mex warehouses in the province of Córdoba, causing a fire of Dantesque proportions, which ended up consuming four million litres of fuel. Six people died in the attack on the Shell warehouses, prompting the government to increase raids and security measures, dividing the country into operational zones and establishing military courts to prosecute those responsible.

The most despicable terrorist act carried out by this organisation took place in the early morning of 12 March of that year, when a terrorist *Uturunco* commando placed an explosive charge of 6kg of TNT in the house of State Information Service (SIDE) Army Major David René Cabrera in La Lucila, in the province of Buenos Aires. The attack on Major Cabrera's home had a tragic conclusion when rescuers extracted the body of 3-year-old Guillermina, the third of Major Cabrera's four children, from the rubble of the house, which was completely demolished. The group thus inaugurated a cowardly and infamous way of waging war, attacking civilian targets, without weighing up the consequences. Guillermina died on the spot and her 5-year-old brother, Gerónimo Luis, was seriously injured. Cabrera's wife, Celmira Rojo Jurado, suffered bruising, as did their other children, 8-year-old Mario and 6-month-old María Elina. The operation was apparently planned by Alberto Campos, with the explosives supplied by a militant named Juan Carlos Brid and the attack carried out by a commando group headed by Héctor Rodolfo Gringoli and two other men. Two days later, they blew up the Mar del Plata gas plant.

Faced with the wave of arrests that were being made, members of the Peronist Resistance and the *Uturuncos* began to disperse.

Ejército Guerrillero del Pueblo (EGP) (1963–1964)

In June 1963, a Guevarist guerrilla group known as the People's Guerrilla Army (*Ejército Guerrillero del* Pueblo/EGP), led by

Causa Honda Indignación Pública el Brutal Atentado Terrorista

CON UNA BOMBA FUE VOLADA LA CASA DE UN MILITAR: MURIO UNA NIÑITA DE TRES AÑOS

El Mayor Cabrera Alcanzó a Ver un Auto Negro, Ocupado por 4 Personas, que Arrancó al Ocurrir el Estallido

Victima Inocente

Sigue Desplazándose Velozmente Hacia el Sol el "Pionero V"

DEMOCRACIA

Testimonio Elocuente del Criminal Atentado

The front page of the newspaper *Democracia* on 13 March 1960 announcing the deplorable *Uturunco* terrorist act (left). Major Cabrera's house before the attack (centre), and what was left of the Cabrera family home after the bomb blast (right). (Open Source)

Jorge Ricardo Masetti interviewing Che Guevara (left) and Fidel Castro (right) in Sierra Maestra, Cuba, in 1958. (Open Source)

Jorge Masetti, leader of the EGP (left) and the EGP flag (red over black with 'EGP' in white) (right). (Open Source)

Jorge Ricardo Masetti, known as *Segundo Comandante* (Second Commander, the First Commander being Che Guevara), was created with the support of Cuba. Masetti, who was born in Avellaneda in 1929, was an Argentine journalist who had worked for the Cuban press agency *Prensa Latina*. He was known previously for his ultra-right leanings and militancy in the fearsome *Alianza Libertadora Nacionalista*, where he associated with Rodolfo Walsh and Rogelio García Lupo. However, after interviews he conducted with Fidel Castro and Che Guevara in Sierra Maestra, Cuba, for Radio *El Mundo* of Buenos Aires, his political beliefs moved to the left. Masetti was fascinated by both leaders, and especially the movement they led, becoming in a matter of days a determined supporter of the revolutionary cause.

Che summoned Masetti to organise a guerrilla group whose purpose was to raise dissent in the Argentine northwest and launch the revolution in his native country. Masetti took the lead, aided by the Cubans Hermes Peña, Juan Alberto Castellanos, José María Martínez Tamayo (known as *Papi*) and Abelardo Colomé Ibarra (known as *Furry*), and the Argentine Ciro Roberto Bustos (known as *Pelao*). After acquiring a farm near the Emboruzú River in Bolivia as an operational base, they began to gather weapons, ammunition and equipment.

They made an incursion from Bolivian territory into Argentina in what they called *Operación Penelope*, establishing themselves in the province of Salta. The guerrillas wandered in the remote region, characterised by its inhospitable countryside, poisonous insects, snakes and wild animals, uninhabited areas and having practically nothing to hunt. With the passage of time, the guerrillas began to languish, there were several desertions, and hunger and disease began to make themselves felt. The group was soon located by the local Gendarmerie and the Salta Provincial Police and there were some clashes, with six guerrillas killed and 14 captured. The end of this pathetic incursion was in accordance with its ephemeral existence; Masetti, accompanied by Atilio Altamirano, managed to evade pursuit, entered the Yuto jungle and then disappeared without trace, the pair presumably meeting their end while fleeing from the security forces. The imprisoned guerrillas were taken to San Ramón de la Nueva Orán and thrown into jail awaiting prosecution and sentencing. They were accused of arms smuggling, possession of ammunition and explosives, homicide and conspiracy to promote a rebellion.

Members of the New Argentina Movement (MNA) guard the DC-4 of *Aerolíneas Argentinas* after landing at a horse racetrack in Port Stanley on the Falkland Islands on 28 September 1966. (*Diario La Nación*)

Operativo Cóndor (1966)

Operation Condor[3] was an armed action carried out on 28 and 29 September 1966 by a group of 18 right-wing Peronist nationalists, members of the New Argentine Movement (*Movimiento Nueva Argentina*/MNA). The MNA were led by Dardo Manuel Cabo, a journalist, who had been a member of *Tacuara*, would later join the *Descamisados* command and finally the *Montoneros*. The group boarded *Aerolíneas Argentinas* flight AR648 in Buenos Aires, bound for Río Gallegos, as regular passengers. The aircraft was a Douglas DC-4, registration LV-AGG, christened *Teniente Benjamín Matienzo*, with 42 passengers and six crew members.

When the DC-4 was flying between Comodoro Rivadavia and San Julián, members of the group got up from their seats and threatened the passengers with guns that they had hidden in their luggage. They demanded that the pilot, Captain Ernesto Fernández García, and First Officer Silvio Sosa Laprida fly them to the Malvinas Islands (the Falklands, a British overseas territory in the South Atlantic). The flight engineer was the mechanic Aldo Baratti. The islands were covered by low clouds and the pilot could not locate Port Stanley Airport, but after finding a break in the clouds, he made a successful landing on an 800-metre-long horseracing track. Once there, the hijackers raised an Argentine flag, took some islanders (trading as kelpers) hostage and demanded that the governor of the

The DC-4 of *Aerolíneas Argentinas* at the horse racetrack in Port Stanley, Falkland Islands (left). Some of the hijackers raised the Argentine flag in Port Stanley (right). (*Diario La Nación*)

MNA hijackers pose with an Argentine flag (left). The leader of the group, Dardo Manuel Cabo (right). (Open Source)

The Argentine Navy transport ship ARA *Bahía Buen Suceso* took the hijackers and passengers to the city of Ushuaia. (Histarmar Archives)

Once the crisis was over, the *Aerolíneas Argentinas* DC-4 was an attraction for the kelpers in their routine and peaceful life. It took 10 days to get the runway ready for the aircraft to take-off. (*Diario La Nación*)

Falklands, Cosmo Haskard, recognise Argentine sovereignty over the islands.

Police and military personnel stationed on the islands surrounded the aircraft, ordering the hijackers to surrender. The island's Catholic priest, Father Rodolfo Roel, acted as mediator in the negotiations. Hours later, and after arduous discussions, the hijackers left their weapons on board the DC-4 and, together with Father Roel, all went to the Catholic church in Port Stanley. Later, they were escorted to the Argentine Navy ship ARA *Bahía Buen Suceso*, moored in Port Stanley's harbour, together with the rest of the DC-4 passengers. They were then all transported to the city of Ushuaia in Tierra del Fuego, southern Argentina. Once there, the hijackers were prosecuted by the courts for the crimes of 'qualified personal deprivation of liberty' and 'possession of weapons of war', the hijacking of airplanes not being contemplated in the Argentine legislation of the time. They were all sentenced to prison. Most of them were released after nine months, with the exception of Dardo Cabo, Alejandro Giovenco and Juan Carlos Rodríguez, who, due to their criminal records, spent three years in jail.

As for the hijacked DC-4, due to its weight, the landing gear sank into the soft ground at Port Stanley Airport. With hard work on the part of the islanders and the use of wooden planks, the aircraft was eventually pulled out of the mud. Ten days after landing on the islands, and after inspecting the makeshift runway, the crew managed to take-off without any problems. Once airborne, the DC-4 was escorted by an Argentine Naval Aviation Grumman Albatross to the Río Gallegos Naval Air Base, where it finally landed.

Fuerzas Armadas Peronistas (FAP) (1967–1979)

This rural guerrilla movement, Peronist Armed Forces (*Fuerzas Armadas Peronistas*/FAP) originated in early 1967 and comprised militants from the Peronist Youth. During the second semester of 1968, 18 guerrillas, including one woman, settled in La Caña, located southeast of San Miguel de Tucumán, 120km from the town of Taco Ralo, where they proceeded to establish a camp. The group was made up of Juan Bertelli, Samuel Leonardo Slutzky, Carlos Alberto Caride, Gerardo Ferrari, Carlos Edgardo Olivera, Arturo Ferré Gadea, José Luis Rojas (known as *Comandante Zupay*), Hernán Aredes, Néstor Herdinsky, David José Ramos, Hugo Ernesto Petenatti, Orlando Zelli, Juan Luis Lucero, Benicio Ulpiano Pérez, Néstro Raúl Verdinelli (*Comandante Sabino*), Amanda Beatriz Peralta de Dieguéz (*Negra*), Félix Francisco Serravalle (*Comandante Puma*) and their commander, Envar El Kadri (*Cacho*), who had been one of the main mentors of the FAP, to which the group belonged. His aim, like that of the *Uturuncos*, was to launch a revolutionary war

FAP members in Tucumán towards the end of the 1960s (left). FAP leader Envar El Kadri (right). (Open Source)

FAP guerrillas when they were captured in Taco Ralo, Tucumán in 1968 (left). Two versions of the FAP emblem (right). (Open Source)

FAR leaders, from left to right, Marcos Osatinsky, Francisco Urondo, Roberto Quieto and Carlos Olmedo. (Open Source)

Garín's branch of the *Banco de la Provincia de Buenos Aires*, with its walls painted with the initials of the FAR, in 1969 (left). A public march of FAR sympathisers in Buenos Aires in the late 1960s (centre). The emblem of the FAR (right). (Open Source)

in order to teach the people the true path to their liberation and demand the return of Perón for later elections.

Having chosen the place for the camp, which the guerrillas called *El Plumerillo*,[4] they proceeded to dig a series of trenches, established hiding places to store their weapons, erected tents and began training exercises to acclimatise to the terrain. The only confrontation they had took place less than a month later, on the night of 18 September, when 60 members of the Provincial Police, under the command of Commissioner Hugo Tamagnini and Major Ramón Eduardo Herrera, head of the division at the provincial level, surrounded the camp. Upon reaching La Caña, the police force divided into two sections, proceeding to encircle the camp and cut off its exits. They avoided the line of trenches that surrounded it, seized the arsenal and, when they were discovered, opened fire. The exchange of shots lasted barely 15 minutes and ended with the arrest of nine guerrillas and the escape of the remaining five, who were captured the following day, discovered hiding in the surrounding countryside.

The insurgents were taken to Taco Ralo police station and then to Tucumán, where the press was able to take pictures of them. The police seized two trucks that had been painted green, weapons of various calibres, ammunition, explosives, uniforms, blankets, clothing, supplies and 500,000 pesos in bills. They were able to determine that the group was called the *Comando 17 de Octubre* and that it belonged to the FAP, founded in April of that year, by elements of the Peronist Youth. It was also learned that their plans were focused mainly on the mountainous region of Aconquija, where the group intended to move once the training period in the plain had finished, and that they planned to make Tucumán their centre of operations, to expand the fight towards Catamarca, Salta and the entire northwest of Argentina. Obviously, the conditions were not yet ripe to unleash a civil war in Argentina, since the insurgents still did not have enough support, their training was poor and the conditions adverse.

Fuerzas Armadas Revolucionarias (FAR) (1967–1973)

The Revolutionary Armed Forces (*Fuerzas Armadas Revolucionarias*/FAR) was an armed political organisation formed in Argentina in March 1967, whose early goal was to train and join the rural guerrillas started by Che Guevara in Bolivia. Its original basic ideology was therefore Marxism-Leninism.

On 26 June 1969, FAR members set on fire 13 Minimax supermarkets in Buenos Aires, in response to a visit to Argentina by American businessman and politician Nelson Rockefeller. But it was on 30 July 1970 that the FAR carried out its first important attack, seizing Garín, a town of 30,000 inhabitants located 35km north of Buenos Aires, on the road to Escobar. This guerrilla group was headed by Marcos Osatinsky (known as *Lucio*), Roberto Jorge Quieto (*Negro*), Francisco Urondo (*Paco*), Carlos Enrique Eduardo Olmedo (*Germán*), Juan Julio Roqué (*Iván*) and Juan Pablo Maestre, whose plan for the attack on the town was inspired by the takeover of Pando by the Uruguayan guerrilla group called *Tupamaros*.

The FAR guerrilla command had drawn up plans for what it termed *Operación Gabriela*, which consisted of assaulting the Garín branch of the Bank of the Province of Buenos Aires, the police station, the home of civilian radio amateur Bruno Torasso (who possessed a transmitter they wished to silence), the local branch of ENTEL (*Empresa Nacional de Telecomunicaciones*, Argentina's main telephone company) and Garín railway station. To achieve all this, the FAR disposed of a total of 36 troops (24 men and 12 women) and about eight vehicles, of which at least three were used to establish surveillance posts and to close the main accesses of the town. Initially, all went well, but when they got to the bank, they killed a police guard. Some of the town's residents, realising what was happening, raised the alarm and police officers from other cities arrived in Garín to confront the guerrillas. In an exchange of fire, a woman living in the town was fatally wounded and the guerrillas, overwhelmed by the firepower of the police, aborted their plan and fled in vehicles in different directions, but not before leaving a large number of pamphlets in the town to make themselves known to the populace and announce their objectives, which included repudiating the 1955 coup against Perón and its innocent victims, the 1956 executions and the capture and murder of guerrillas in the 1960s.

The news once again shocked Argentine public opinion, which was increasingly concerned, having witnessed acts of political violence taking place with worrying frequency, without the authorities being able to prevent them. Once made aware of the attack, President General Levingston called his cabinet to analyse the situation. They decided to rigorously apply repressive regulations already in force, making use of the powers granted by a state of siege, which included the death penalty.

The following year, the FAR struck again. On 29 April 1971, they attacked a military truck on a street in Pilar to steal weapons, comprising 193 .45-calibre Ballester Molina pistols and 344 magazines, with their respective ammunition. One member of the attackers, Sara Solarz de Osatinsky, killed Lieutenant Mario César Asúa during the attack. Then in October of that year, the FAR raided a private home, stealing communication equipment. That same month, they attacked a quarry in Juárez Celman, Córdoba, seizing explosives, and also assaulted the Pueyrredón Cooperative in Córdoba, stealing money.

Argentina was undoubtedly now at war. The insurgent groups described their actions as being part of a war, and referred to it as such in their communiqués, making it clear that extremely difficult times were coming for the nation.

FAR guerrilla Sara Solarz de Osatinsky (left) who assassinated Lieutenant Mario César Asúa (right) in Pilar on 29 April 1971 when attacking an Army truck to steal weapons. (Open Source)

Fuerzas Argentinas de Liberación (FAL) (1968–1973)

Although some future members of the FAL (*Frente Argentino de Liberación* or *Fuerzas Argentinas de Liberación*/Argentine Liberation Front, Argentine Liberation Forces or Argentine Forces of Liberation) started to meet and organise in 1962, it was not until 1968 that their subversive attacks began, with minor actions – such as assaults on bank branches to raise funds and seizures of police stations to obtain weapons – and in some cases sporadic seizures of small towns, mainly in the provinces of Buenos Aires and Santa Fé. This Marxist-Leninist ideology organisation was divided into three components: FAL *22 de Agosto*, FAL *Ché Guevara* and FAL *29 de Mayo*. The last two groups, with power mainly in Córdoba and Santa Fé, would eventually be integrated into the ERP.

In April 1969, the FAL seized a bivouac of the Argentine Army's Patricios Regiment in the Campo de Mayo base, stealing weapons. The FAL at this time was made up of six groups: those dissatisfied with the Communist Youth Federation headed by Hernán Jorge Enríquez; the Peronist Revolutionary Youth of the MRP, led by Gustavo Rearte; the Workers' Revolutionary Party, *El Combatiente* sector; the Revolutionary Socialists, who went over to the Trotskyist Revolutionary Workers Party (PORT); the Communist Vanguard (VC), with a Maoist tendency; and the Revolutionary Communist Party (RCP), also influenced by Mao's thoughts. Two of the FAL's founder members were Juan Carlos Cibelli and Jorge Pérez.

In May 1969, the Federal Police arrested two members of the FAL, Alejandro Baldú and Carlos Della Nave, on suspicion of organising an attack on a train that was carrying cash. The insurgents feared the pair had been killed by the police, and on 24 March 1970, two FAL militants kidnapped the Paraguayan consul in Ituzaingó, Waldemar Sánchez, while he was in Buenos Aires, in order to force the police to publicly show Baldú and Della Nave. The police showed Della Nave to the press and the consul was promptly released by his captors.

Comando Descamisados (1968–1972)

The 'Shirtless Commando' (*Comando Descamisados*) was a Peronist guerrilla organisation that operated in Argentina between 1968 and 1972. It was founded in 1968 by Horacio Mendizábal, Norberto Armando Habegger and Fernando Saavedra Luque. In 1969, Dardo Manuel Cabo became the commander of the organisation. Among the actions carried out by this group were the blowing up of the Tigre Naval Circle boat club and the yacht of the Commander-in-Chief of the Navy, the kidnapping of the manager of the General Electric-

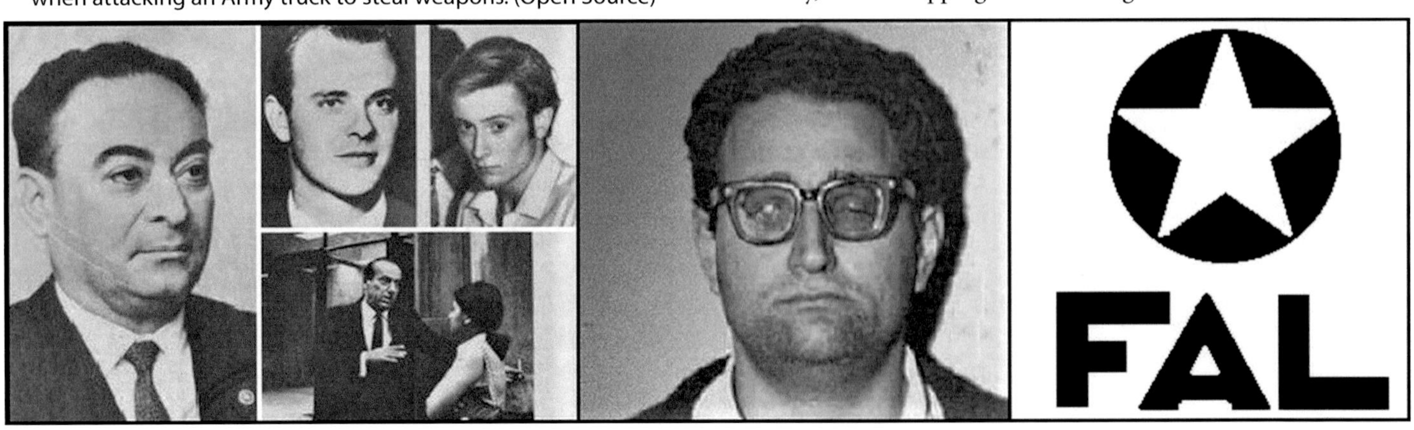

The Paraguayan consul in Ituzaingó, Waldemar Sánchez, who was kidnapped by the FAL (left). Two members of the FAL were caught by the police, Alejandro Baldú and Carlos Della Nave. One of the founders of the FAL, Juan Carlos Sibelli (centre), and the emblem of the FAL (left). (Open Source)

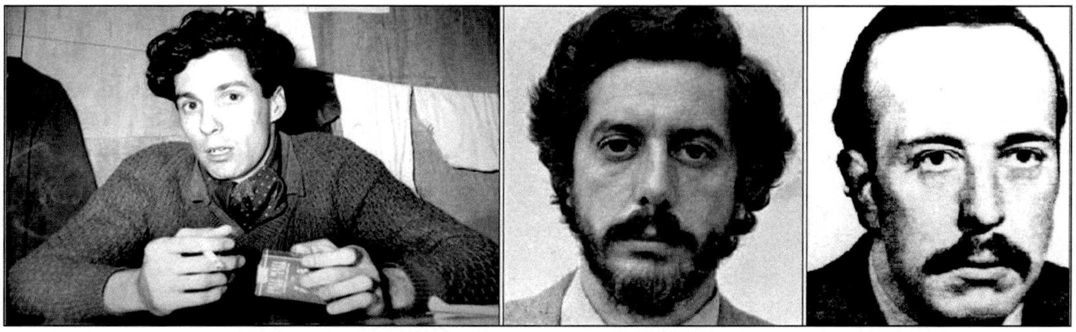

Some of the leaders of the Shirtless Commandos. From left to right, Dardo Manuel Cabo, Horacio Mendizábal and Norberto Habegger. (Open source)

The emblem and slogan normally used by the *Descamisados*. The 'P' over the 'V' meant 'Perón Returns', and the inscription indicated 'fight and he will return'. (Open Source)

Union leader Augusto Vandor, assassinated by the *Descamisados* (left). Vandor's office, destroyed by a bomb (right). (Open Source)

ITT company of San Isidro – for whose ransom they collected a million dollars – and robberies at several financial institutions. On 30 June 1969, they carried out *Operación Judas*, assassinating the union leader Augusto Timoteo Vandor at the headquarters of the Metallurgical Workers Union (UOM) and then blowing up a bomb in his office. The *Descamisados* considered Vandor a traitor to the workers' cause, which was why the operation was called 'Judas'. In 1972, the *Descamisados* joined the *Montoneros*.

The key year of 1969

From 1966, Lieutenant General Juan Carlos Onganía, head of the Argentine Revolution (*Revolución Argentina*) movement, which had overthrown President Arturo Illia, ruled the country. The Onganía government achieved a level of stability for the nation rarely accomplished in Argentine history. The country's external debt was minimal and barely moved within normal rates, and school dropout levels were almost nil, as was unemployment. Argentina's currency remained stable during the four years that the government held power, exports grew and prices stabilised, which made healthy competition possible. Furthermore, the nation's GDP grew by 5 percent, inflation remained below 8 percent and the balance of payments obtained a surplus of US$200 million. The rates of public services were frozen and the CONADE (National Development Council) was created, aimed at promoting the integral development of the country, promoting the production of the private sector with the manufacture and export of goods. This stability was what allowed the working classes to buy houses in instalments and pay for them with such ease that, in the end, their obligations ended up costing them 'less than a pack of cigarettes', according to the popular saying of the time. In this way, even the proletariat also had access to motor vehicles, loans, household appliances, health care, vacations and other benefits that had not been seen since the days of Perón, although much less publicised. In addition, no matter how much authoritarianism, prohibition and censorship there was, in those years members of the populace were not being killed or disappearing at the hands of the government, as has been claimed by some.

In the technological and scientific field, the impulse that the regime gave to the nation was considerable. In December 1967, the RA-3 Research and Production Reactor was inaugurated in Atucha; the following year, construction of the Atucha I Grand Nuclear Power Plant began. Almost at the same time, work began on the El Chocón-Cerros Colorados hydroelectric complex, the great Zárate-Brazo Largo bridge, the El Nihuil II hydroelectric dam in Mendoza, the Balcarce Satellite Earth Station and the subfluvial tunnel that connects Santa Fé with Paraná.

Lieutenant General Juan Carlos Onganía when he assumed the *de facto* presidency of Argentina on 29 June 1966. (Open Source)

Despite all the positive developments for Argentina at this time, the *Cordobazo* took place on 29 and 30 May 1969, a violent strike by workers and students in Córdoba promoted by the CGT and the Argentine University Federation. The strikers were confronted by troops of the III Army Corps, reinforced by the IV Airborne Infantry Brigade, Air Force troops, members of the Gendarmerie and the Federal Police. The troops were greeted with shots, stones, bottles, bolts (thrown with slingshots) and Molotov cocktails, but faced with their firepower, the protesters had no choice but to give in and withdraw, but not before 17 demonstrators were killed and at least 400 wounded. The clashes and skirmishes turned into open confrontations, even making use of firearms. State institutions such as the Ministry of Public Works, the NCO Club (*Círculo de Suboficiales*), the offices of Gas del Estado, the *Banco del Interior* and offices of entities linked to US capital such as Xerox, Tecnicor, Burroughs and the headquarters of the Jockey Club were stoned, as were shops, premises and market stalls. Then there were two general strikes in Rosario in September, known as the *Rosariazo*, and likewise the *Tucumanazo* in Tucumán. All these riots were stimulated by the Peronist Resistance and severely weakened the unelected *de facto* government. As a consequence, Onganía was replaced by another *de facto* regime headed by General Roberto Marcelo Levingston on 18 June 1970.

In the time of Onganía, thousands of kilometres of roads, bridges, dikes and dams were built, access to the federal capital and the main cities of the country were improved, investments were made to modernise the railway service (tracks, signals, and the replacement of wagons and old locomotives with versatile and much more dynamic Fiat ones run by fuel oil) and studies began for the construction of the Gualeguaychú-Fray Bentos bridge and, together with Paraguay, the Yacyretá-Apipé hydroelectric power plant.

At the Military Aircraft Factory (*Fábrica Militar de Aviones*/FMA) of Córdoba, important undertakings were developed such as the IA.58 Pucará attack combat aircraft, the first flight of which took place in 1969. In missile and space matters, various achievements were obtained by the FMA, placing the country among the only six nations on Earth committed to the exploration of outer space and just three that made launches from the Antarctic continent.

The first prototype of the FMA IA.58 Pucará, serial AX-01, being built at the Military Aircraft Factory in Córdoba in 1969. The famous Pucará would have its baptism of fire in the war against the guerrillas in Tucumán in 1975. (*Area de Material Córdoba, Fuerza Aérea Argentina*)

Above, the popular protests in the city of Córdoba, known as the *Cordobazo*, in May 1969. Below, the *Rosariazo* in Rosario in September of the same year. On the right, the riots in San Miguel de Tucumán in September, known as the *Tucumanazo*. (Open Source)

Montoneros (1970–1980)

The word *Montonero* comes from *montón* (lot) and refers to a person who fights together with others. The original *Montoneros* were the nineteenth century *gauchos* who had fought with the Argentinian heroes of independence for emancipation from the decadent domain of the Spanish crown. The name was taken up by a Peronist subversive/terrorist organisation which emerged in the first months of 1970. Its base ideology was left-wing revolutionary Peronism. It was formed by the fusion of several Peronist armed groups with Catholic roots. At least initially, it was organised in two commandos and four groups, as follows:

Commandos Camilo Torres: The *Montoneros* named its Commandos in honour of the Catholic Father Camilo Torres, a Colombian priest who later became a guerrilla. Two commands were established:

Commando Camilo Torres of Buenos Aires: The so-called 'Founding Group'. Towards the end of 1969, the leader was Fernando Abal Medina and its other leading members included Carlos Ramus, Norma Arrostito, Mario Firmenich, Carlos Alberto Maguid and Graciela Daleo.

Commando Camilo Torres of Córdoba: Its main members were Emilio Maza, Ignacio Vélez, Héctor Araujo, the priest Alberto Fulgencio Rojas, Liprandi, Susana Lesgart, Alejandro José Yofre, Carlos Capuano Martínez and José Fierro.

Sabino group: José Sabino Navarro (known as *El Negro*) was a union member of SMATA (*Sindicato de Mecánicos y Afines del Transporte Automotor*/Union of Mechanics and Related Automotive Transport). He formed a guerrilla group in January 1969, which also included José Amorín, Hilda Rosenberg, Gustavo Lafleur, Carlos Hobert, Graciela Maliandi, Tito Veitzman and Carlos Falaschi.

Reconquista Group: This was based in the city of Reconquista and operated mainly in the north of the province of Santa Fé, and to a lesser extent in Tucumán and Salta. It was represented

Gallery of *Montonero* leaders. Top row, from left to right, Mario Firmenich, Fernando Abal Medina, Roberto Perdía, Capuano Martínez and Carlos Gustavo Ramus. Bottom row, from left to right, Emilio Maza, Fernando Vaca Narvaja, Norma Arrostito and Roberto Quieto. (Open Source)

by Roberto Perdía and also included Hugo Medina, Ricardo Nadalich and Juan Belaustegui.

Santa Fé Group: Based at the *Ateneo de Santa Fe*, it was led by Mario Ernst and included René Oberlín, Roberto Rufino Pirles, Osvaldo Agustín Cambiasso, Raúl Clemente Yagger, Raúl Bracco, Juan Carlos Menesses, Marcelo Nívoli, Carlos Legaz and Fernando Vaca Narvaja.

Córdoba Group: Its main members were Alberto Molina, Luis Rodeiro and the priest Elvio Alberione.

The *Montoneros* was established as a political-military organisation (*Organización Político-Militar*/OPM), its intention being to be considered one of the existing organisations within the Peronist Movement, led by Juan Domingo Perón. This would change after Perón's death, first with the creation of the Authentic Peronist Party (or simply Authentic Party) in 1975 and then with the founding of the *Montonero* Party in 1976.

One of the first and most violent actions of the *Montoneros* was the kidnapping and subsequent assassination of former president Lieutenant General (Retired) Pedro Eugenio Aramburu, which took place on 29 May 1970 in *Operación Pindapoy*, with the idea of submitting him to a revolutionary court to avenge the executions of June 1956. They also wanted to recover the corpse of Eva Perón, which the Liberating Revolution had made disappear the previous year. The aim was for the kidnap and execution of the former president to publicise the existence of the group. Operation Pindapoy was meticulously planned, at least a year before, and even preceded the existence of the *Montoneros*. The participants, after locating the apartment where Aramburu lived, studied his daily routine and the different options to carry out the kidnapping. Ironically, the decision was made to carry out the mission on Argentine Army Day, celebrated every 29 May. Two *Montoneros* guerrillas disguised as army officers, a captain (Emilio Maza) and a lieutenant (Fernando Abal Medina), appeared in uniform at General Aramburu's apartment in Buenos Aires, asking to speak with him. They claimed that the Argentine Army had assigned them as bodyguards for the former president. As they talked, they drew their weapons and forced the general to go with them. At that time, the *Montoneros* movement still had fewer than 20 members. The commando group that carried out the mission comprised Mario Eduardo Firmenich, Norma Esther Arrostito, Ignacio Vélez, Emilio Maza, Carlos Alberto Maguid, Fernando Abal Medina, Carlos Ramus, Carlos Raúl Capuano Martínez and two others. Aramburu was taken to a ranch in Timote, in the province of Buenos Aires, a property of the Ramus family, prosecuted by a 'popular' court and executed on 1 June. The charges put to Aramburu were the proscription of Peronism, the theft and mutilation of the corpse of Eva Perón, the executions of Peronists (military and civilians) in June 1956 and having an anti-popular economic policy. At 7:00 a.m. on 1 June, the head of the commando, Fernando Abal Medina, fired three shots at Aramburu with a 9mm pistol, then shot him again with a .45 pistol. The corpse was buried in the basement of the ranch house.

Former president Lieutenant General (Ret.) Pedro Eugenio Aramburu in 1970, the first victim of the *Montoneros*. (Open Source)

Once the crime had been carried out, the *Montoneros* issued a statement for the public, taking responsibility for the kidnapping and execution of Aramburu. Wasting no time, the government reacted by putting into effect the national security doctrine that Lieutenant General Onganía had implemented when he took office, including capital punishment for crimes of this nature. Special forces of the Federal Police, in collaboration with their provincial counterparts, began a search and the intelligence services set out to find those responsible. A firm response had to be made to reassure the public, and immediately, because a new form of violence was taking over the nation and terrorism was beginning to prevail; a terror unknown before then.

Only a month later, the *Montoneros* struck again, taking over the town of La Calera. Using various vehicles, heavily armed *Montoneros* stormed the town's police station. They captured the deputy commissioner and attacked the town's telephone exchange, rendering it inoperative. The group then assaulted the branch of the *Banco de la Provincia de Córdoba*. A police officer who was passing by the bank was wounded by the *Montoneros*, but he managed to escape and raise the alarm to the commander of the III Army Corps. Together with the IV Airborne Infantry Brigade, they set out to block all local roads in order to capture the guerrillas. Two *Montoneros* were taken and interrogated, providing valuable information with which it was possible to capture 12 more of the subversives, along with weapons, explosives and documentation. During the confrontation, one of the founders of the *Montoneros* group, Emilio Maza, was mortally wounded. Over the

Several *Montoneros* leaders at a meeting in the early 1970s (left). The official emblem of the *Montoneros* (right). (Open Source)

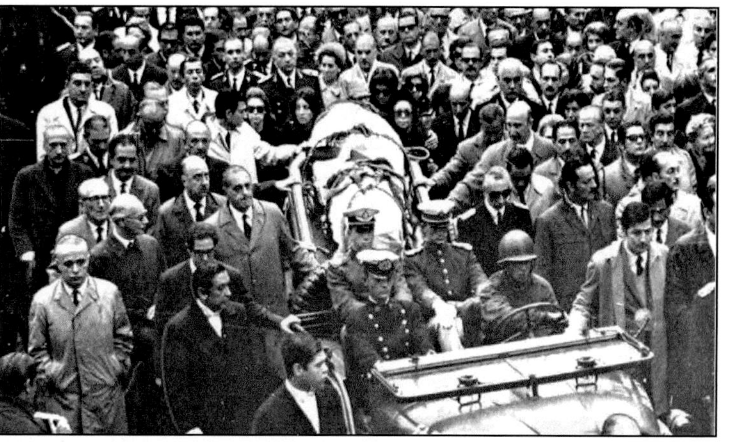

The funeral of former president Aramburu. On the left, the son of Aramburu together with Army Commander Lieutenant General Alejandro Agustín Lanusse next to the coffin. There was a massive turnout of people at the state funeral for Aramburu (right). (Open Source)

Union leader José Alonso with his wife in 1970. (Open Source)

following days, another 10 *Montoneros* were captured, severely disrupting the Córdoba section of the organisation.

It was only on 17 July that year that the body of General Aramburu was found by personnel of the Argentine Federal Police. It had been possible to locate the exact place thanks to declarations made by *Montoneros* captured in Córdoba. Aramburu's remains were taken to his home on Montevideo Street in Buenos Aires and then to *La Recoleta* cemetery. A large crowd gathered to accompany the procession to the funeral. The coffin with the mortal remains of the former president was pulled by a military vehicle, preceded by a detachment of horsemen from the Grenadier Regiment. The highest national, ecclesiastical, civil and military authorities carried the coffin, led by the President of Argentina, General Roberto M. Levingston, and the Commander-in-Chief of the Army, General Alejandro Agustín Lanusse. During the burial, after Monsignor Juan Carlos Aramburu's response, Admiral (Retired) Isaac Francisco Rojas, who was vice-president for the deceased between 1955 and 1958, spoke to the congregation, as did General Bernardino Labayru and General Lanusse.

The remaining *Montoneros* managed to evade capture by the security forces after the assassination of Aramburu and the taking of La Calera, and with the support of sympathisers, they managed to regroup and swiftly return to action. During August, the group attacked the Laguna Larga branch of the *Banco del Interior y Buenos Aires*, stealing 27 million pesos, and at the beginning of September carried out another operation against a bank in the province of Buenos Aires, taking several million more pesos. In a statement they issued after the first robbery, they promised further actions and reprisals for the death of Emilio Maza, making it clear that they were serious.

Their next blow was much bloodier and more resounding. Since Augusto Vandor's death in 1969, José Alonso had become the most powerful trade unionist in Argentina. A tailor by profession, he was one of the creators of the Garment Industry Workers Union (SOIVA), founded on 23 March 1943, from which, following the guidelines of the Justicialist leader, he managed to neutralise the Garment Workers Federation (FOV), which was infiltrated by socialists, communists and 'undesirable elements'. In 1946, Alonso became a member of the coordinating table of the General Confederation of Labour (CGT), which he represented at numerous international congresses. In 1952, Alonso won a seat in Congress as a representative for the federal capital, a position he held until 1955 when the military overthrew Perón's regime. He went into exile in Venezuela before returning to the country during the Frondizi government. He then became the General Secretary of the CGT. In the mid-1960s, Vandor's faction removed him from the leadership of the CGT. Towards the end of the 1960s, the *Montoneros* targeted Alonso, accusing him of being a fascist and a traitor to the proletarian cause. The group's leadership decided to execute him after a plenary meeting. In the heart of the city of Buenos Aires, on 7 August 1970, Alonso's car was intercepted by two vehicles driven by *Montoneros*, who blocked his path. They then got out of their vehicles and shot the union leader, seriously wounding him before finishing him off with six more shots. Within hours, the Emilio Maza Command of the *Montoneros* claimed responsibility for the act.

Further violent actions were carried out by the *Montoneros* in 1970. On 1 September of that year, a *Montonero* commando group assaulted the *Banco Galicia* branch in Ramos Mejía, taking $13,750,000 pesos. The operation lasted less than 10 minutes and was coordinated by Fernando Luis Abal Medina, with Carlos Gustavo Ramus acting as his deputy. That same day, the insurgents seized an Uzi submachine gun, two 9mm Browning GP35 pistols and a long-barrelled .32-calibre revolver. A week after the bank robbery in Ramos Mejía, the *Montonero* leadership planned a meeting in William C. Morris, northwest of Greater Buenos Aires, to resolve two things: the appointment of Luis Enrique Rodeiro as operational head of the organisation in Córdoba, in place of the fallen Maza, and to discuss with Antonio Romano the financing of the organisation so as to receive a large sum of money from him. However, they made a fatal mistake. Instead of meeting privately, they chose a popular pizza parlour. Fernando Abal Medina, Luis Enrique Rodeiro, Carlos Gustavo Rasmus, José Sabino Navarro, Norberto Rodolfo Crocco and Carlos Capuano Martínez arrived there at around 8:30 p.m. They were all carrying guns and even hand grenades. The owner of the pizza parlour recognised some of the *Montoneros* and discreetly called the police. Almost immediately, an officer and three heavily armed NCOs sped to the scene in a patrol car. Upon the police arriving and identifying the *Montoneros*, the insurgents drew their weapons but the policemen were faster, managing to mortally wound Abal Medina. Ramus reacted by trying to fire his machine gun and throwing a grenade but was shot and fatally injured. Rodeiro then surrendered and the others fled. During Abal Medina's funeral, attendees and the press could clearly see a wreath bearing the name of Juan Domingo Perón.

Three leaders of the PRT-ERP, from left to right, Mario Roberto Santucho, Benito Jorge Urteaga and Enrique Gorriarán Merlo. The PRT flag (red field with yellow star and lettering) (above) and the ERP flag (white over light blue with a red star and white lettering) (below). (Open Source)

There were further attacks carried out later in 1970. On 9 October, the *Montoneros* attacked the 24th Police Station in Rosario, killing two police NCOs. On 14 October, they assassinated Federal Police Deputy Commissioner Osvaldo Sandoval, who had headed the investigation into the death of former president Aramburu. Finally, on 29 December, two *Montoneros* – Firmenich and Amorín – attacked a police booth in the vicinity of the Olivos presidential residence, killing a policeman and stealing his FMK-3 submachine gun.

Although the *Montoneros* organisation was mainly an urban guerrilla, during *Operativo Independencia* it provided logistical and tactical support to the ERP in Tucumán.

Ejército Revolucionario del Pueblo (ERP) (1970–1976)

The *Partido Revolucionario de Trabajadores* (Revolutionary Workers Party/PRT) was founded on 25 May 1965 in Buenos Aires from the merger of two political groups: the *Frente Revolucionario Indoamericanista Popular* (Popular Indo-American Revolutionary Front/FRIP) and *Palabra Obrera* (Worker Word/PO). This came about through the relationship of Mario Roberto Santucho from the FRIP with Leandro Fote, a sugar union leader member of the PO. Its ideological base was heterodox, with a mixture of Trotskyist, Guevarist, Castrist, Leninist and Maoist principles. The PRT managed to infiltrate elements in unions, factories, state offices, universities and political parties.

On 29 July 1970, the Fifth Congress of the Revolutionary Workers Party (PRT) took place on an island in the Paraná River delta, attended by the main leaders of the national Trotskyist left. During the event, Mario Roberto Santucho, known as *Roby*, one of its founders, presented a programme, prepared together with former *Tacuara* member José Baxter (*Joe*), in which he proposed armed struggle to achieve power. Among those present were Enrique Gorriarán Merlo, Luis Enrique Pujals, Benito Jorge Urteaga, Domingo Menna, Jorge Carlos Molina, Luis Mattini, Miguel Ángel Polti, Santucho's wife Ana María Villarreal, Asdrúbal Santucho and Clarisa Lea Place. At the congress, the armed wing of the PRT was founded, which received the name of the People's Revolutionary Army (*Ejército Revolucionario del Pueblo*/ERP). Santucho was appointed commander of the ERP, having received guerrilla training in Cuba in 1961. The new group's main objective was to create a rural guerrilla focus in Tucumán, a sort of 'Argentine Vietnam'.

During the last semester of 1970, the ERP dedicated itself to consolidating its structure and establishing a plan of struggle, aimed at raising funds and obtaining weapons. Its operations began in January of the following year, with an attack on the 24th Police Station in Rosario and an assault on the National Institute of Agricultural Technology (INTA) in Metán, in the province of Salta, where the group appropriated a typewriter and a mimeograph. In Rosario, it assaulted the Telcom repair shop, seizing communications equipment, and during the following days overpowered several law enforcement officers to seize their weapons. A few days later, however, the police arrested several of its members, including Domingo Menna, Alicia Quinteros, Hugo Alberto Sosa and Eduardo Potti, the latter injured when the house where he was sleeping was searched. Despite these arrests being a severe blow, the nascent force still had enough energy to continue its action, first by taking over the facilities of the construction company Argentina Vosin S.A., on Route 36, in the province of Córdoba, seizing four uniforms, five revolvers and portable transistors.

In February, the ERP assaulted several armouries and stole large quantities of weapons. The following month, they took over the San Lucas private clinic in the San Isidro neighbourhood of Buenos Aires, stealing medical supplies to set up clandestine health posts for the guerrillas. During April, the ERP launched the first issue of *Estrella Roja* (Red Star) magazine, its official organ, a clandestine publication, printed on stolen mimeographs, through which it announced its action programme, its intention to form support commandos and their military actions. On 17 April, the police killed three ERP militants – Marcelo Lezcano (known as *Pelado*), José Alberto Polti and Juan del Valle Taborda – who at the time of being intercepted were driving a recently stolen Ford F-100 pick-up truck. In May, the ERP attacked both the Tobacco Chamber building and the Telesima Argentina company in Ensenada with explosives. They also kidnapped Stanley Sylvester, the British manager of Swift Refrigeration Industry, requesting the massive distribution of food in poor neighbourhoods as ransom, in an action of political propaganda.

On 11 July, the ERP took over the *Buen Pastor* (Good Shepherd) Women's Prison in Córdoba, releasing several detained terrorists. Some days later, they attacked the home of an executive chief of the Fiat company with explosives.

Cover of the first edition of the ERP's *Estrella Roja* magazine, published and distributed clandestinely. (Open Source)

Throughout August, ERP members were very active with the seizure of the Gonnet police station, stealing armaments and police uniforms. They did the same at a police station in Salta. On 8 August, they tried unsuccessfully to kidnap Lieutenant General (Retired) Julio Alsogaray in Buenos Aires. Later that month, they launched a bomb attack on a building under construction to house military personnel in Rosario. In September, they attacked the car of an executive director of the SUBPGA meat processing plant with explosives. They also stole money from the Tucumán Telephone Company and took over Villa Urquiza Prison, releasing 14 terrorist prisoners, killing five prison guards in the process. During the same month, the ERP bombed the Fray Luis Beltrán police station in Santa Fé and the Brajkovic company in the same city, along with the Alba Paint Company and the Molinos Río de la Plata, both in Rosario.

On 11 October, the ERP seized the civil registry office of Villa Carmela in Tucumán and stole documents, stamps and typewriters for the manufacture of false documents for terrorists. Occasionally, the ERP would also take over a public square or a school for a few hours with the purpose of raising the flag of the guerrilla organisation, and then flee when state forces approached. Many of their assaults were merely for the purpose of obtaining money and/or weapons for the organisation, rather than to cause injury or death.

The *Viborazo* and the fall of the Levingston government

On 2 March 1971, the government of General Levingston appointed José Camilo Uriburu as federal comptroller of the province of Córdoba, which was not well received by unionists and students. During the National Wheat Festival in Córdoba, Uriburu mentioned a phrase that would trigger a violent protest: 'Confused among the multiple mass of moral values that Córdoba by definition is, nestles a poisonous Marxist snake whose head I ask God to grant me the historical honour of cut in one fell swoop.'[5] His mention of 'a poisonous Marxist snake' gave rise to massive protests that were later called the *Viborazo* ('The big snake').

Union leaders summoned the workers of major industries such as *Grandes Motores Diesel*, Fiat, Perkins and Thompson Ramco to a

The violent protests in Córdoba in 1971 known as the *Viborazo* (left). The comptroller of the province of Córdoba, José Camilo Uriburu (right, in a light suit), together with the *de facto* President General Levingston (centre). (Open Source)

Brigadier General Roberto Marcelo Levingston, *de facto* President of Argentina for only nine months, between June 1970 and March 1971. (*Revista Panorama*)

Lieutenant General Alejandro Agustín Lanusse, *de facto* President of Argentina between 1971 and 1973. (Open Source)

massive protest on 12 March, which was joined by students of the Peronist Revolutionary Youth, socialists and even ERP militants. It was said that Santucho himself was among the protesters. The government, in response, mobilised the police and placed Army, Air Force and Gendarmerie troops on alert in their bases. ERP infiltrators incited violence among the masses of workers and students, and the fuse that ignited the explosion was a shot fired by a police officer that mortally wounded one of the students. The crowds reacted by throwing stones, bottles and lumps of iron, and the police responded with tear gas. The masses took over several neighbourhoods of the city, even attacking supermarkets, banks and the Jockey Club. They set fire to shops and cars, causing chaos in the city. The central government sent the Anti-Guerrilla Brigade of the Federal Police, which arrived at the provincial capital headed by the fearsome Commissioner Alberto Villar. The forces of law and order again had the support of the paratroopers of the IV Airborne Brigade and members of the Army, who entered the city at night to dislodge, one by one, the barricades, pushing protesters outside the occupied neighbourhoods.

The mass protests greatly weakened the already weak government of General Levingston. On 22 March, Levingston dismissed the Army Commander, Lieutenant General Alejandro Agustín Lanusse, who responded the following day by leading a palace coup that ousted the president from power.

Lanusse government (1971–1973)

The armed forces of Argentina had notably not been seriously involved in the fight against subversion during the governments of Onganía and Levingston. Some have interpreted this as the wicked intention of Army Commander Lieutenant General Lanusse to weaken those governments, but as of March 1971, Lanusse was the *de facto* President of the Republic. Through Law 19,053 of 28 May of that year, the Federal Criminal Chamber was created to pass judgement on guerrilla and terrorist activities, in order to combat the problem of the guerrillas within the framework of the law. This made it possible for the authorities to capture, try and imprison around 2,000 guerrillas in the early 1970s, out of almost 9,000 cases brought to court.

A joint operation by the FAR, the FAP and the *Montoneros* resulted in the killing of Major Julio Ricardo San Martino, former police chief and current director of the Penitentiary Service of the province of Córdoba, who was accused by the terrorists of being one of the instigators of the repression against workers during the *Vivorazo* protests. He was targeted at 1:15 p.m. on 29 July 1971 when he was returning to his home in Alta Córdoba.

At 4:30 p.m. on 6 September 1971, a combined force of the ERP and the National Liberation Army (*Ejército de Liberación Nacional*/ELN) attacked Villa Urquiza Prison in the city of San Miguel de Tucumán, to free political detainees who were held there. Taking advantage of the recreation period at the jail, the inmates took over one of the weapons stores, grabbing pistols and revolvers, then ran to the guard room to overcome its occupants. The prisoners were led by Ramón Rosa Jiménez, known as *Zurdo*, one of the founders of the ERP. The insurgent assault group then quickly entered the prison, and with the support of the inmates seized the lobby, two adjoining units and the administration block, killing three policemen. As they left the building, a further confrontation took place, in which three more prison guards were injured. The rebels barely suffered any casualties as they withdrew, boarding a gas truck and several vehicles parked nearby to make good their escape. Twenty-four inmates were released, although only 18 managed to escape, including José Benito Urteaga and Ramón Rosa Jiménez. José Ricardo Mena, Segundo Suárez and four other companions remained inside the jail, and a few days later were transferred to Rawson Prison.

In early November, another incident took place on the outskirts of Córdoba that left four subversives dead and at least one detained after a joint action by the *Montoneros*, the Revolutionary Armed Forces and the Peronist Armed Forces. At the end of the previous month, the three organisations had begun to draw up a risky plan with the aim of kidnapping a senior executive of Fiat. At 6:00 a.m. on 3 November, two private vehicles parked on the side of Route 9 in front of the ESSO service station, near the access to the Fiat industrial complex, waiting for the executive in question. In command of the operation was Carlos Enrique Olmedo (known as *Germán*, *José* or *El Rubio*), assisted by Agustín Villagra (*Tin*), dressed in police uniforms. A third vehicle nearby contained other rebels, while a fourth car was following the Fiat executive's vehicle. However, workers at the ESSO service station became suspicious of the parked vehicles and called the police. When patrolmen arrived

Oberdán Sallustro, General Director of Fiat Concord Argentina, during his captivity after being kidnapped by the ERP in Buenos Aires. (Open Source)

at the scene to check the vehicles, there was a confrontation in which two of the insurgents were killed and the others fled.

During 1972 and 1973, insurgent and guerrilla actions notably increased, but the government's military response was also more forceful. From 1971, with the creation of the Federal Criminal Chamber, the authorities were able to effectively control and neutralise the criminal activities of the rebels.

During 1972, several major attacks were launched by the *Montoneros*. On 1 January, they took over the Naval Prefecture of Zárate and stole many weapons. Two weeks later, they bombed the house of former Justice Minister Jaime Perriaux, who had created the Federal Criminal Chamber to deal with terrorist acts, killing a police officer. On 18 January, they killed Roberto Mario Uzal, the political leader of the *Nueva Fuerza* Party as he was leaving his home in Olivos. That same day, they assassinated the Principal Commander of the National Gendarmerie, Pedro Agarotti, the former Chief of Police of Tucumán, at his residence in Quilmes.

As for the ERP, its attacks were their bloodiest in 1972. On 10 January, the group took over the National Development Bank and stole several million pesos. One ERP action that was widely covered by the press was the kidnapping on 21 March of businessman Oberdán Guillermo Sallustro D'Amato, an Italian-Paraguayan citizen and General Director of Fiat Concord Argentina. While driving to his office, he was intercepted by two vehicles containing guerrilla commandos, who forced him to go with them. Sallustro's driver, who was wounded by the guerrillas, managed to reach his boss's house, where relatives alerted the police. The commando group comprised eight guerrillas, three of whom were women. They were headed by Osvaldo Debenedetti and supervised by Joe Baxter, but also included Mario Raúl Klachko (known as *Polaco*), Benito Urteaga, Roberto Coppo and Klachko's wife, Guiomar Schmidt. Other direct participants in the Sallustro kidnapping were Ángel Averame (known as *Gordo*), Elena Codan, Carlos Tomás Ponce de León, José Luis Da Silva Parreira, his sister Elena María and his wife Mirta Adriana Mitidiero, all members of the PRT-ERP. Sallustro was taken to a private house in the Lugano neighbourhood of Buenos Aires, behind which was a 'people's jail' (a place where leftist activists kept those who had been kidnapped), where they kept him locked up. Forty-eight hours later, they issued a statement demanding the release of political prisoners, improvements in Fiat's working conditions, the reinstatement of laid-off workers, the repeal of repressive laws and a million-dollar ransom. This kidnapping caused a shock not only in Argentina but also in Italy. Indeed, Fiat directors in Italy sent a representative to negotiate the ransom payment and the release of Sallustro. However, it was all in vain as the guerrillas, upon realising they had been discovered by the police, shot their hostage dead with four bullets on 10 April. The assassin was Mario Raúl Klachko.

The same day, under the code name *Operación Sonia Segunda*, combined guerrilla forces of the ERP and FAR assassinated Army Major General Juan Carlos Sánchez in Rosario, while he was travelling to the city of Santa Fé in an Army Ford Falcon with his driver, NCO Celestino Barneche, to carry out an inspection visit. The attack also killed a civilian woman, Elcira Cucco de Araya, who was at a newsstand nearby. Sánchez was the commander of the II Army Corps and an expert in anti-subversive operations. The assassination was carried out by FAR leader Juan Roqué, known as *Lino*, who would later join the *Montoneros*, and *Montonero* first officer Martín Gras (*Cacho*). The government posthumously promoted General Sánchez to lieutenant general and the II Army Corps was named after him in his honour.

Some days later, the ERP launched a bomb attack on members of the IKA company board of directors. Then on the 27th, they took over the police

Another victim of the ERP, on this occasion in combination with the FAR, was Major General Juan Carlos Sánchez, Commander of the II Army Corps (left). General Sánchez's Ford Falcon car is shown after the attack (right). (Open Source)

Rawson Prison, where numerous insurgents were imprisoned (left). Trelew Airport, where the *Austral* BAC One-Eleven was hijacked (right). (Open Source)

The BAC One-Eleven 521FH, registration LV-JNS, of *Austral Líneas Aéreas*, which was hijacked by guerrillas who escaped from Rawson Prison. (Esteban Raczynski Collection)

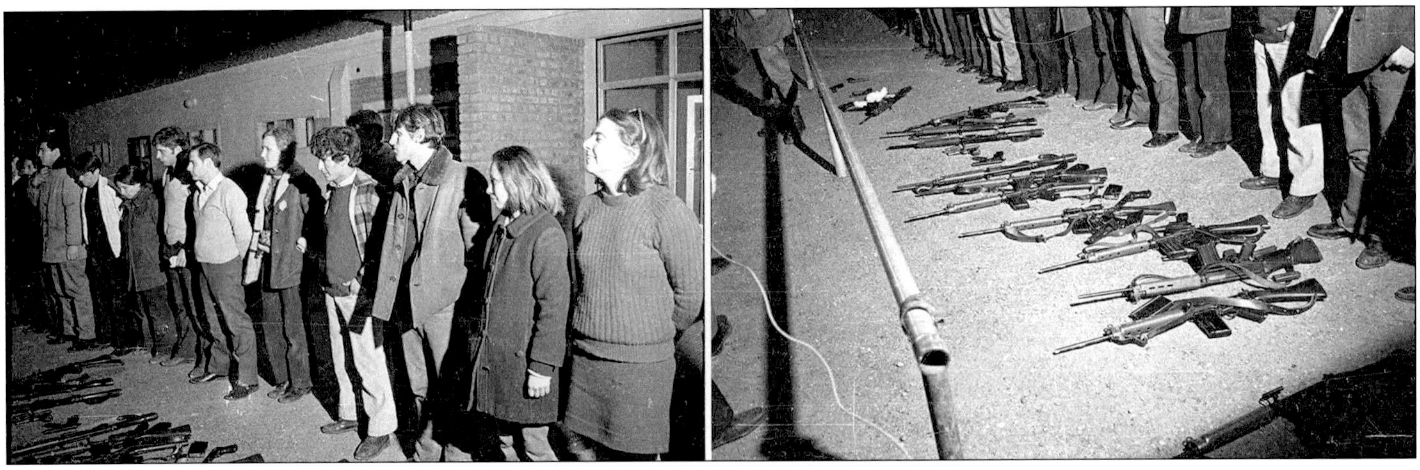

Some of the second group of guerrillas who did not manage to board the hijacked aircraft. They finally surrendered to Marine Infantry troops that had surrounded Trelew Airport (left). The weapons of the captured subversives (right). (Open Source)

detachment building in Río Tala, in the province of Buenos Aires, killing one police officer and stealing numerous weapons. On 1 May, they seized a detachment of the Naval Prefecture in Dock Sur, Buenos Aires, again stealing weapons.

On 15 August, ERP, FAR and *Montoneros* guerrillas who were serving sentences in Rawson Prison, Chubut, carried out a major escape, in a planned joint action with the participation of their defence lawyers, who had provided them with weapons. The terrorists who escaped included Roberto Santucho (ERP), Roberto Quieto (FAR), Marcos Osatinsky (FAR), Carlos Goldenberg (FAR), Fernando Vaca Narvaja (*Montoneros*), Domingo Menna (ERP) and Enrique Gorriarán Merlo (ERP). The escape was helped by almost all the prison guards having been bribed by terrorist threats against their wives and children, along with the management of the prison. When the terrorists fled, some of the prison guards resisted, two of them, J. Galarraga and J.G. Valenzuela, being killed with shots to the head by Ana María Villarreal de Santucho, who had been unable to escape.

The first group of escapees fled to Trelew Airport, where another terrorist group, disguised in Army and Gendarmerie uniforms, had already hijacked the *Austral Líneas Aéreas* BAC One-Eleven 521FH, registration LV-JNS, and taken all the crew members and passengers as hostages. The regular *Austral* flight number AU-811 had departed from Comodoro Rivadavia Airport earlier that day and was to stop at Trelew and Bahía Blanca, with its final destination being Buenos Aires. The flight deck crew comprised Captain Eduardo Ford and First Officer Abelardo Calay, with 96 passengers and three flight attendants, Nora Peirano, María Pizarro and Cora Walsoe. Some guerrillas who were disguised as passengers – Alejandro Ferreyra Beltrán, Víctor Fernández Palmeira and Ana María Weissen – were already on board and carrying weapons, and once they landed at Trelew they went to the flight deck, threatening the pilots. The group of seven guerrillas boarded the aircraft and ordered the pilots to take-off immediately, leaving 19 of their comrades behind, fearing repressive action by the local Army, Navy and police forces.

Once in the air, the pilots were requested to fly to Puerto Montt in Chile, where they landed at El Tepual Airport around 9:30 p.m. Immediately after refuelling, the BAC One-Eleven departed again, bound for Santiago, where it landed shortly before midnight. The Austral jet would return with all its passengers to Buenos Aires on 16 August.

Once the second group of guerrillas arrived at the airport, they entrenched themselves in the passenger terminal building, taking air terminal employees as hostages. Before the terrorists occupied the airport control tower, air traffic controllers managed to divert an Aerolíneas Argentinas Boeing 737-200 from Comodoro Rivadavia that was due to land there. As soon as the news spread that a group of prisoners had escaped from the prison, the authorities initiated repressive action, mobilising forces from the three armed services, as well as security forces (the Prefecture, Gendarmerie, Provincial Police and firefighters), closing all access to the airport and setting up roadblocks.

The Argentine Air Force dispatched a C-130 Hercules from Comodoro Rivadavia with troops from the 8th Mechanised Infantry

Above, the guerrillas captured at Trelew Airport were taken in trucks escorted by Marines (left) to the Almirante Zar Naval Air Base (BAAZ) (right). The 16 subversives killed in the Naval Air Base when they supposedly attempted to escape (below). (Open Source)

Regiment under the command of Lieutenant Colonel Alberto Podestá, while in Bahía Blanca an Aero Commander AC500 was pressed into service for General Eduardo José Ignacio Betti, chief of the XI Infantry Brigade, recently appointed military commander of the region (now declared an emergency zone), to travel to the crisis zone, accompanied by members of his staff. Furthermore, Marine Infantry troops of the 4th Marine Battalion, under the command of Frigate Captain Rubén Norberto Paccagnini, also arrived and surrounded the area, leaving the second band of guerrillas with no option but to surrender. They were taken to Almirante Zar Naval Air Base in Trelew, given the now widely acknowledged lack of security at Rawson Prison. In vain, President Lanusse requested the extradition of the guerrillas in Chile to his counterpart Salvador Allende, who instead granted them safe conduct to request asylum in Cuba on 25 August. They were taken to Cuba on a *Cubana de Aviación* Ilyushin aircraft. As a consequence of this decision, Argentina withdrew its ambassador in Chile and presented a protest note to the Chilean government.

According to the official version of events, at 03:30 a.m. on 22 August, at the Almirante Zar Naval Air Base, the 19 detainees made a dramatic bid for freedom, Mariano Pujadas taking hostage an officer of the Navy, Corvette Captain Luis Emilio Sosa. However, Sosa managed to escape from his captors and threw himself to the ground between the terrorists and their armed guards, ordering them to open fire. As shots rang out, 16 of the terrorists were killed, with the three others being seriously injured. None of the Navy personnel were injured. The surviving guerrillas gave another version of what happened. According to their testimony, the 19 detainees were suddenly woken up and taken out of their cells. They were then lined up, forced to face the ground and were machinegunned by a group of Marines led by Corvette Captain Sosa and Lieutenant Roberto Bravo. Most of the insurgents died immediately, with some of the wounded being finished off by sidearms as they lay helpless on the floor. When the shooting ended, the three survivors were taken to the infirmary, but no medical assistance was provided. They were transferred the following day to Puerto Belgrano Naval Base, where their wounds were taken care of. Upon reading the news of the killings, Perón, still in exile, described the incident as 'premeditated murder'.[6]

Those killed were: Alejandro Ulla, Carlos Alberto del Rey, Ana María Villarreal de Santucho, Clarisa Lea Place, Eduardo Capello, Humberto Suárez, Humberto Toschi, José Ricardo Mena, Mario Emilio Delfino, Miguel Ángel Polti and Rubén Pedro Bonnet (all PRT-ERP members); Alfredo Kohan, María Angélica Sabelli and Carlos Astudillo (from the FAR); and Mariano Pujadas and Susana Lesgart (*Montoneros*). The wounded, who managed to survive the massacre and who testified about the events, were later killed by subsequent military governments. They were Alberto Miguel Camps (FAR, killed in 1977), María Antonia Berger (FAR, disappeared in 1979) and Ricardo René Haidar (*Montoneros*, disappeared in 1982).

There were numerous other incidents in 1972. On 9 November, members of the FAR kidnapped metallurgical businessman E. Barrella in Buenos Aires and asked for a ransom of five million dollars. On 9 December, the ERP attacked with explosives the home of the owner of the Norglas factory in Tucumán. The following day, the ERP kidnapped the meatpacking businessman Ronald Grove and asked for a ransom of a million dollars. Grove was released, but two days later, the FAR killed retired Rear Admiral Emilio Rodolfo Berisso in Lomas de Zamora, in retaliation for the events in Trelew. He was shot in the back when he was leaving a supermarket with his wife. His killer was a young man who got out of a Ford Falcon and approached him from behind, firing three shots at short range. The officer fell to the ground, where he received two more shots. His assailant fled in the same car in which he had arrived.

In 1972, the government of General Lanusse announced that democratic elections would be held on 11 March 1973 and the

Dr Héctor Cámpora of the Justicialist Party (left) won the 1973 elections against Dr Ricardo Balbín of the Radical Civic Union (right). (Open Source)

handover of power would take place on 25 May. It was imposed as a condition that the candidates had to be in the country before 25 August 1972 and remain within the country until the date of the presidential inauguration. Perón, still in exile in Spain, refused these conditions and instead gave his blessing to Dr Héctor Cámpora to present himself as a candidate for the Justicialist Party in the elections.

The last months of the Lanusse government were marked by guerrilla violence. In the early morning of 3 January, a 15-strong commando group of *Montoneros*, including four women, tried to seize the Zárate detachment of the Argentine Naval Prefecture, on the Paraná River. The guard reacted immediately, leading to an intense firefight, and managed to repel the guerrilla attack, with injuries on both sides. On 14 January, the first major attack by the FAL in the Argentine insurgency war took place when a powerful explosive device destroyed the home of Minister Jaime Perriaux in Buenos Aires. The blast killed two policemen instantly and seriously injured two more who would die later, destroying the first two floors of the building and causing damage to nearby buildings. Neither Dr Perriaux nor his family were at his home when the attack took place. On the 29th, the ERP carried out a spectacular assault on the National Development Bank (BANADE) in Buenos Aires, from which it stole 450 million pesos, the highest figure appropriated by the guerrillas until that point.

On 19 February, the ERP took over the base of Army Communications Battalion 141 in Córdoba. The ERP leadership was aware that the bulk of the unit, some 640 men, was on manoeuvres beyond Alta Gracia, in José de la Quintana, having left 36 hours earlier under the command of Lieutenant Colonel Luchessi. Remaining in the barracks was only a token guard, made up of 60 troops, under the orders of a major. The attack was launched by six ERP squads – *29 de Mayo*, *Che Guevara*, *Lazcano-Polti-Taboada*, *Jorge Luis Sbedico*, *Ramiro Leguizamón* and *Martínez-Ferreira* – with 40 men wearing military uniforms. They had stolen a large quantity of weapons (250 machine guns, automatic rifles, machine pistols, grenade launchers and semi-automatic pistols) in the city of Córdoba to use in the assault. They were able to easily get into the base thanks to a conscript who was a member of the terrorist organisation.

Days before the elections, the Federal Police seized documentation from the FAR revealing details of Operation *Corina*, through which it was planned to sink the Argentine Navy submarine ARA *Santiago del Estero* (S-22) at its base in Mar del Plata, using explosives placed under its hull by divers. In addition, the group was planning to blow up numerous charges at a nearby golf club and a commando group would occupy Necochea police station to seize weapons.

The elections were held on 11 March, the successful candidate being Héctor Cámpora of the Justicialist Party (PJ) with 49.53 percent of the first ballot votes. Ricardo Balbín, from the Radical Civic Union (*Unión Cívica Radical*/UCR), achieved a weak second place with 21.29 percent, and Francisco Manrique, the candidate of the government for the Federal Party (PF), obtained third place, but without reaching the 15 percent that would have allowed him to go to the second ballot. A few days later, Balbín announced that he would not run in the second round and Cámpora was proclaimed president.

On 12 March, an ERP commando group tried to take over the guard at Morón Air Base, an important Air Force facility, home of the VII Air Brigade, killing a soldier who tried to prevent the attack. A few days later, the ERP killed the main commander of the Gendarmerie, Pedro Abel Agarotti, who had been the Gendarmerie Chief in Tucumán. The *Montoneros* also murdered the political leader and lawyer Roberto Mario Uzal in his own home. One of the subversives was fatally wounded by Uzal before the target was shot to death.

On 15 March, an ERP platoon seized weapons in Longchamps, then on the 17th several more bombs were detonated, one of them in the home of the owner of Sugarosa, an important meat refrigeration company in Rosario, and another in San Jorge Military Equestrian Club, located in the area surrounding Hurlingham, a joint action undertaken by a *Descamisados* detachment, the *Montoneros* and the FAR.

On 30 March, the ERP tried to place a bomb in the Navy Command's Libertad Building in the federal capital. Navy conscript

Argentine Navy Submarine ARA *Santiago del Estero* (S-22) setting sail from its base in Mar del Plata in the 1970s (left). The same submarine is shown moored at Mar del Plata (right). (Histarmar Archives)

Rear Admiral Francisco Alemán during his 68-day captivity in an ERP 'people's jail' in 1973. (Open Source)

Dirck Henry Kloosterman, engineer and union leader, general secretary of the Union of Mechanical Workers (SMATA) of the CGT, was assassinated by FAP subversives. (Open Source)

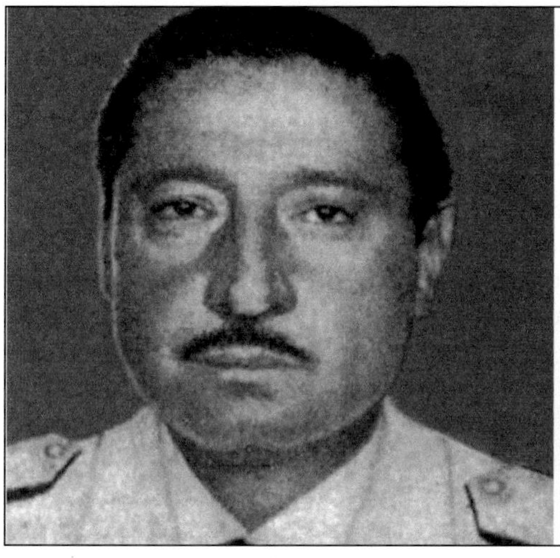

Rear Admiral Hermes José Quijada, who was murdered by the ERP (left). When he was a frigate captain in 1962, he commanded an air expedition to the South Pole with a pair of Douglas C-47s. Quijada is in the centre of the photo with other naval aviators (right). (*Gaceta Marinera*)

Julio Provenzano, a member of the terrorist group, died when the bomb he was handling exploded in a bathroom. Two days later, the ERP kidnapped Rear Admiral D. Francisco A. Alemán. His own nephew, Oscar Ciarlotti, who was the son of a Navy captain, and Magdalena Nosiglia were in charge of this action. The admiral was kept in a 'people's jail' for 68 days before being released.

On 30 April, the ERP killed naval aviator Rear Admiral Hermes Quijada under Operation Mercury (*Operación Mercurio*). His car was intercepted by two subversives on a motorcycle, who shot him to death, and a car with other four terrorists. One of the terrorists on the motorcycle, Víctor José Fernández Palmeiro (known as *Dedo* or *Gallego*), was killed by the admiral's driver, 1st Corporal Rufino Ocampo, who was lightly wounded. Quijada was promoted to the rank of admiral *post-mortem*.

In the days prior to the inauguration of President-elect Dr Cámpora, there were several attacks by guerrilla organisations. On 22 May, the FAP assassinated Peronist union leader Dirck Henry Kloosterman in the province of Buenos Aires. That same day, they tried unsuccessfully to kidnap a Swift company executive, a Mr Volinsky. The following day, Luis Giovanelli, an executive of the Ford motor company, was assassinated and a Mr Bellinson of the Babic company was kidnapped for ransom.

Thus ended what people in general thought was the 'last' *de facto* government of Argentina, and it was believed that with the legally elected Cámpora government, the terrorist actions of the guerrillas would disappear. However, such hopes collapsed immediately, as rather than diminishing, the guerrilla attacks increased dramatically.

2
CÁMPORA, LASTIRI, PERÓN AND PERÓN, 1973–1976

Between 25 May and 12 October 1973, a period of less than five months, Argentina had three presidents. Then from 1 July 1974 to 24 March 1976, María Estela Martínez de Perón was in charge of the government, but as she proved unable to solve the country's economic crisis, and above all the serious problem of the guerrillas, the military deposed her and installed a dictatorship.

Cámpora's term

Dr Héctor José Cámpora, known as *El Tío* ('The Uncle'), took office on 25 May 1973, thus ending the *de facto* period of the self-proclaimed Argentine Revolution. His vice-president was Vicente Solano Lima. The inauguration ceremony was attended by, among others, the then socialist President of Chile, Salvador Allende, and that of Cuba, Osvaldo Dorticós. Cámpora belonged to the Peronist left and his two sons were *Montoneros* supporters. A huge crowd, estimated between 200,000 and 700,000 people, occupied the area between the Congress and the *Casa Rosada* to celebrate the end of 18 years of *de facto* military regimes. The crowd was angry at the three commanders who made up the Military Junta, insulting them and smashing the windows of the car carrying Brigadier Carlos Rey, Commander of the Air Force, and physically assaulting Admiral Carlos Coda, accusing him of the Trelew massacre. Guards repelled the attack by firing shots, seriously wounding 12 people. Despite this, there were no further incidents, and while Rey and Coda withdrew by helicopter, former president Lanusse did so by car. The *Montoneros* infiltrated the crowd and painted the backs of soldiers in the security cordon with aerosol paint, and also military vehicles, and the scheduled military parade was cancelled.

With the people filling the streets, the democratic government had to face its first conflict that same day as a result of the massive demand for the release of political prisoners of the *de facto* regimes, something that Cámpora had committed himself to in his electoral campaign. By the time Cámpora was sworn in as president, shortly after noon, there was already unanimity in Congress that the amnesty should be broad and include all political prisoners, including the guerrillas. However, the leftist groups demanded the release of their comrades that same day, going to the various prisons without waiting for the official order of liberation. Chaos ensued, in which several demonstrators died. To avoid further bloodshed, Decree 11/1973 was issued the following day, providing for the pardon of 372 subversives, some of whom were serving life sentences. On 27 May, the National Congress unanimously sanctioned Law No. 20,508, providing amnesty for all political crimes, including those committed due to or on the occasion of a strike, factory occupation or other measure of force. The Penal Federal Chamber was dissolved, thereby encouraging the guerrillas, who became more violent. President Cámpora and all the legislators had thought that a general amnesty would lessen and eventually bring to an end the political violence of previous years, but they were very wrong. General Perón, who was still in Spain, did not like this measure at all.

Cámpora's brief government was characterised by having Marxist elements in high positions, including governorships and ministries, with parliament having the support of Third World Catholic priests, left-wing university professors, artists and journalists.

Cámpora appointed Lieutenant General Jorge Raúl Carcagno as the new commander of the Army, with Brigadier General Héctor Luis Fautario heading the Air Force and Admiral Carlos Álvarez the Navy. The three military commanders belonged to the 'professional integrationist' sector of the armed forces, which maintained that the military should always be subject to democratic civil power. During Cámpora's short government, there was a truce with the *Montoneros*, with several of the group's members appointed to important positions in the state, but the ERP continued its campaign of attacks without any stoppage.

Cámpora's government lasted just 49 days, from 25 May until 13 July 1973. In that short period of government, numerous acts of terrorist violence were carried out around Argentina by guerrilla organisations. Things started promisingly, however, when on 29 May the FAR freed the kidnapped businessman Enrique Fridman, manager of *Mecánica Lanín* after receiving a ransom. Then a few days later, another kidnapped businessman, Oscar Caster, manager of Coca Cola, was also liberated after the receipt of a ransom. On 2 June, though, the ERP took over the Bonelli Metallurgical Company in Córdoba, stealing weapons. Two days later, the FAR killed Peronist

Dr Héctor José Cámpora (centre, with the presidential sash) with all the members of his cabinet, including the commanders of the armed forces, on the day of his presidential inauguration on 25 May 1973. (Open Source)

General Perón and President Cámpora met with *Generalissimo* Francisco Franco in Madrid before returning to Argentina in 1973. (Open Source)

trade union leader Pascual Almada. On 6 June, the ERP assaulted the headquarters of the Army Radioelectric Command in Merlo; one of the terrorists, Luis Castrogiovanni, was seriously wounded in

Perón and Cámpora descending from the Boeing 707 of *Aerolíneas Argentinas*, which landed at Morón Air Base instead of Ezeiza International Airport due to the shooting among those attending the planned reception. (Open Source)

the attack and later died. That same day, the ERP also kidnapped for extortion the executive Carlos Lockwood, later receiving a ransom of 2.3 million pesos.

The Ezeiza massacre. Right-wing Peronist union leaders brandishing guns on stage (top left), attendees from the Peronist left (top right), members of the press taking cover during the shooting (bottom left), and armed civilians among those attending the event, panicked by the shooting. (*Diario Clarín*)

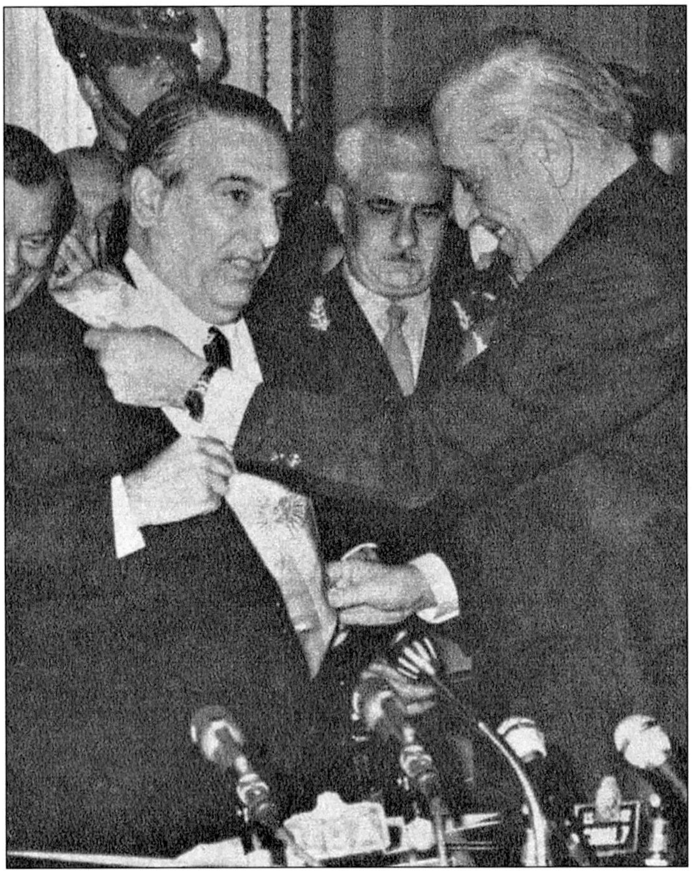

The outgoing President Cámpora, imposing the presidential sash on his successor, Raúl Lastiri, in July 1973. (Open Source)

While all this was happening, Cámpora travelled to Spain to visit Perón and prepare for his eventual return. However, he was furiously admonished by Perón for his government's lack of decisions that favoured the guerrillas. It was established that Cámpora had to resign and new elections were to be called that same year, in which Perón would present himself as a candidate for the Justicialist Party.

Meanwhile, the political violence and guerrilla attacks continued apace. On 15 June, the ERP seized the family home of an executive of the Dalmine Siderca company in Campana, setting off a bomb which practically destroyed the building. That same day, the ERP took over the Dulesnea company in La Plata, stealing milk that was delivered to the poor. Two days later, the ERP kidnapped John Thompson, an executive of Firestone, in Lomas de Zamora, demanding a ransom of one million dollars.

General Perón and his entourage, including President Cámpora, returned to Argentina on 20 June on an *Aerolíneas Argentinas* Boeing 707. They were due to land at Ezeiza International Airport and then make a speech on a stage set up on Bridge 12 at the junction of the Ricchieri highway with Provincial Route 4, about 10km from the airport. Thousands of Peronists had gathered in the area, both from right-wing (mainly CGT union leaders) and left-wing groups (*Montoneros*, FAR and Peronist Youth). Many of them were armed, with the intention of attacking their opponents. Furthermore, the ERP planned to assassinate Perón – the Five Continents Plan (*Plan Cinco Continentes*) – and take over the government. The ERP mobilised 2,000 of its combatants for this. They stationed snipers in trees around the stage, and also intended to use grenades to bring down the helicopter that would transport Perón from Ezeiza Airport. However, Perón's military adviser, Colonel Osinde, upon realising the intentions of the leftist factions, immediately ordered they be neutralised. When the left-wing agitators tried to get closer to the stage, those from the right-wing groups opened fire and a massacre began. According to official figures, there were 13 dead and 365 wounded, but unofficially it is estimated that the dead and wounded reached more than 500 after several hours of shooting. Vice-President Solano Lima informed Cámpora and Perón of the situation by radio communication from the Ezeiza control tower to the pilot, and the decision was made to divert the 707 jet to land at the Argentine Air Force's base at Morón. The Ezeiza massacre was the precursor of what would happen with the formation of the Argentine Anti-Communist Alliance (the Triple A), organised by José López Rega to put an end to the actions of left-wing Peronism.

On 13 July, President Cámpora and Vice-President Solano Lima presented their resignations before the National Congress meeting in the Legislative Assembly (with both chambers together), which approved them and took Raúl Lastiri's constitutional oath as interim President of Argentina. Lastiri, who then called new elections for 23 September 1973, had been the president of the Chamber of Representatives and was López Rega's son-in-law.

Lastiri's term

During the interim government of Lastiri, the FAR, *Montoneros* and ERP continued to kidnap businessmen for ransom, plant bombs and kill policemen and soldiers. On 6 September, the ERP attacked and seized the Army Health Command in the federal capital, with the aim of stealing weapons and medical supplies. Conscript soldier Hernán Invernizzi acted as an inside agent for his insurgent comrades. In the attack on the guard, Lieutenant Eduardo Rusch and conscript soldier Osvaldo Dedged were seriously wounded. A successful operation to take back the Health Command was carried out by forces of the *Patricios* Regiment, whose Deputy Chief, Lieutenant Colonel Raúl

The duo Perón and Perón on the cover of *Asi* magazine in September 1973. (*Revista Así*)

Duarte Hardoy, led his troops from the front and was killed in combat.

General Perón and his wife, María Estela Martínez de Perón, formed the presidential duo for the Justicialist Party in the elections on 23 September, receiving an overwhelming 61.86 percent of the votes. Their new government took office on 12 October.

Only two days after the elections, under the code name *Operación Traviata*, the *Montoneros* killed the General Secretary of the CGT union, the Peronist José Ignacio Rucci, who was riddled with bullets in an open challenge to Perón. Then on the 26th, the same group killed Peronist politician Enrique Grinberg as he was leaving his home in Buenos Aires.

Peronist union leader José Ignacio Rucci with his children (above). Scenes from the murder of Rucci by the *Montoneros* (below). (Open Source)

Between February and July 1973, heavy rains affected the central-western zone of the province of Buenos Aires, causing floods that meant thousands of people had to be evacuated. Hundreds of homes were submerged, crops were lost, roads became impassable, and facilities and machinery were rendered useless. To deal with this natural disaster, *Operación Dorrego* was carried out between 4 and 23 October, involving 3,944 Army soldiers who belonged to the X Infantry Brigade and the I Cavalry Brigade. The planning and direction of the operation were in the hands of General Eduardo Ignacio Betti, with its execution overseen by his peer, General Albano Eduardo Harguindeguy, with the joint participation of 800 members of the Peronist Youth, the youth wing of the *Montoneros* guerrilla organisation, led by Norberto Habbeger, working side by side for the common good.

Repair work soon began on roads, highways and bridges, while sewers and drains were cleaned and routes, canals and pipelines were reconstructed. Structures in poor condition were demolished and others were erected. Many buildings were reconditioned, especially homes, hospitals, and schools, and protective embankments were built. Thousands of victims of the flooding were evacuated and relocated temporarily in fire stations, railway carriages, sheds and sports facilities. Food was brought to the most needy, along with mattresses and blankets, and medical care was provided and donations were distributed. As might have been predicted, however, the Peronist Youth and the *Montoneros* dedicated themselves to proselytising, distributing copies of the magazine *El Descamisado* among the troops and affected residents to take political advantage of the people's tragedy.

Yet Operation Dorrego was a 'ceasefire' to which not all subversive groups adhered. The ERP did not join in the aid mobilisation, nor did the FAP, continuing with their attacks, kidnappings, tortures, assaults on food trucks, disarming of police, taking over of factories and other premises, raising of party flags, bombings and support for strikes and demonstrations.

Perón and Perón's administration

On 2 October, the government announced that before Perón's inauguration, all officials with Marxist affiliation 'or prone to it' should be expelled, both from the ranks of the movement and from trade union offices, provincial and municipal governments.

Perón assumed his third presidency on 12 October 1973, but his hold on power lasted less than nine months as he passed away on 1 July 1974. He was 79 years old and had been very ill. In August 1973, he had suffered a serious cardiac arrest while being operated on for polyps. Due to the state of his health, he did not carry out any electoral campaigning, which was left entirely in the hands of his wife, María Estela Martínez (known as Isabel), and José López Rega. He was no longer the vital figure of before, by now a weak old man, admired by the CGT union leaders of the right but questioned by those of the Peronist left for not carrying out a true socialist

General Perón assumed his third presidency on 12 October 1973 with his wife, María Estela Martínez de Perón, as vice-president. (Open Source)

Victims of the ERP attack on the Azul military garrison. From left to right, Lieutenant Colonel Jorge Roberto Ibarzábal (kidnapped and later murdered), Colonel Camilo Gay and Mrs Hilda Casaux de Gay (both murdered), along with the daughter of the murdered couple. (Open Source)

revolution. Acting as if nothing had changed, the subversive groups continued their terrorist actions with impunity, but Perón was not Cámpora and he fought them relentlessly, enlisting both legal and illegal methods.

At the end of October, the ERP kidnapped Kurt Schmidt, Latin America manager of the airline Swissair. The kidnappers asked for a ransom of $3.8 million, which was paid by the Swiss airline, and a month later Schmidt was released and returned to his home country.

During October 1973, a series of sporadic attacks began, directed mainly against terrorist organisations and in a few cases against politicians from left-wing parties unrelated to terrorism. They were carried out by the new far-right para-police organisation called the Triple A, which was led by the Minister of Social Welfare, José López Rega. This organisation undoubtedly came into being with the knowledge and blessing of General Perón and his wife, although they publicly denied it when questioned by journalists. The attacks' common denominator was the use of the initials 'AAA' (Triple A) in messages left after each event. The first 'official' attack took place on 21 November, the target being the radical senator Hipólito Solari Yrigoyen, who had opposed a Perón bill – the Law of Professional Associations, which granted unlimited powers to trade unionism – as he considered it to be totalitarian, authoritarian and bureaucratic. A bomb planted in his car exploded when the senator started the engine, seriously injuring him. He received immediate help and was rushed to hospital, where he underwent emergency surgery. He survived, becoming a long-time Radical Civic Union activist, still alive and at the time of writing this book he was 90 years old. Days after the attack on Yrigoyen, the Triple A published a long blacklist of people 'to be opportunely assassinated' wherever they were found, including members of leftist political parties, subversive guerrilla organisations, as well as intellectuals, actors, artists, journalists, members of the military and Catholic priests and bishops with sympathies towards Marxism. Some well-known names on the list included actresses Norma Aleandro and Marilina Ross, writer Julio Cortázar, folk singers Horacio Guarany, Atahualpa Yupanqui and Mercedes Sosa, singers Nacha Guevara and Leonardo Favio, actors Víctor Laplace and Federico Luppi and journalist Jacobo Timerman.

On 23 November, a terrible attack took place in which an American businessman and three members of his team lost their lives. The operation was handled by the FAP and resulted in the death of John Swint, general manager of Transax Argentina, a transport company located in the southern part of the city of Córdoba.

On 19 January 1974, the ERP guerrilla organisation, with a commando force of 240 insurgents, attacked the Army tank regiment barracks at Azul, headquarters of the 10th Tank Cavalry Regiment *Húsares de Pueyrredón* (C-10) and the 1st Armoured Artillery Group *Coronel Martiniano Chilavert*, considered to be the best-armed military unit in Argentina. The attack was led by Enrique Gorriarán Merlo and Hugo Irurzún but failed due to the resistance put up by the guard and the support provided by Army and Marine Infantry troops from nearby garrisons. During the raid, the ERP killed Colonel Camilo Gay and his wife, Hilda Casaux de Gay, along with three conscripts, and took prisoner Lieutenant Colonel Jorge Ibarzábal, who was subjected to atrocious torture and was assassinated 10 months later. The ERP suffered three casualties, while two guerrillas captured by the military later disappeared. Perón responded forcefully by appearing on national television and condemning terrorism, blaming, without mentioning his name, the governor of the province of Buenos Aires, Oscar Bidegain, one of the five governors allied to revolutionary Peronism. He also ordered a reform of the Criminal Code to be rushed through the National

President Perón during the commemorative speech on Labour Day on 1 May 1974 (left). The *Montoneros* and their supporters in Plaza de Mayo that day, when orthodox Peronism broke relations with the *Montoneros* (right). (Open Source)

The Catholic priest Carlos Mugica celebrating a mass (left). Father Mugica with people from poor neighbourhoods of Buenos Aires (right). (Open Source)

Congress to toughen sentences for the crimes committed by guerrilla groups.

The rebel groups ignored Perón's warnings, however, and during the first semester of 1974 numerous terrorist acts were carried out. On 14 February, the *Montoneros* killed radical congressman Hipólito Acuña. Some days later, they kidnapped Swift Meatpacking executive A. Valocchia. On 22 March, they also killed the retired Peronist union leader Rogelio Coria. On 4 April, the General Secretary of the CGT's San Nicolás branch, Antonio Magaldi, was assassinated. The same day, they also killed Fiat personnel manager Roberto Kecker. The ERP, meanwhile, kidnapped US cultural attaché Alfredo Laun, who was wounded in the operation. Several days later, the ERP assassinated former Federal Judge Quiroga in Buenos Aires. On 29 April, the group released ESSO union leader Víctor Samuelson after receiving a ransom of 12 million pesos. Samuelson had been in captivity since 12 June 1973.

On 30 April, the ERP took over the town of Acheral in Tucumán, creating a 'liberated zone' in the province and trying to obtain international status as a regular belligerent force. This was the prelude to what was to come in 1975 and the unleashing of *Operativo Independencia* by the government.

During President Perón's speech for Labour Day on 1 May 1974, there was a confrontation between *Montoneros* and orthodox right-wing Peronist leaders. After numerous riots and verbal confrontations, President Perón employed loudspeakers to harshly label the *Montoneros* as 'beardless stupid youngsters', and the insurgents finally dispersed. Furious, disappointed and convinced that they had been betrayed, the *Montoneros* leaders issued the withdrawal order, recommending their people not to respond to any attacks on them. This only inflamed the crowd, which, encouraged by union elements, began to attack them, throwing all kinds of objects at them. It was impossible to avoid the fighting.

The Marxist infiltration of the government caused Perón to take drastic measures and carry out a major purge, also creating a Security Committee comprising the commanders of the armed forces. On 11 May, the Triple A killed the Third World priest Carlos Mugica, a leftist who supported the guerrilla organisations. Another version of events, however, claims that Father Mugica was killed by

One of the last photos taken of the elderly and sick President Perón during the harsh winter of 1974. (Open Source)

the *Montoneros* themselves, since he had distanced himself from them and moved closer to Perón. Mugica did not agree with the violence of the guerrilla group, especially after the murder of union leader Rucci, and Mario Firmenich, one of the *Montoneros* leaders, had developed a particular dislike for the priest.

Meanwhile, President Perón's health was deteriorating every day and he attended practically no official events, delegating functions to the vice-president. On 1 July, President Perón died in the Presidential House at Olivos, suffering a cardiac arrest resulting from aggravation of his chronic ischemic heart disease. The announcement of his death was made to the country by his widow, Vice-President María Estela Martínez, who shortly after assumed the presidency. However, she did not have the charisma of her husband to govern. Some witnesses present in Olivos stated that in the last hours of Perón's life, and knowing his wife very well, he tried in vain

President María Estela Martínez de Perón, still wearing rigorous mourning, greeting people in 1974. (Open Source)

to hand over the presidency to the radical leader Ricardo Balbín, who was a seasoned politician. Isabel was in no way prepared to lead the country, and consequently the crisis in the country accelerated. The government was left in jeopardy due to its incapacity, its savage internal struggles and the growing guerrilla movement, meaning the support it received from the non-Peronist moderate sectors, the armed forces and democratic political parties was of no importance.

María Estela Martínez de Perón's government

The presidency of María Estela Martínez de Perón took place in a very complicated political and economic context, her government being characterised by a persistent deterioration of political and civil liberties, with a significant shift in Peronism towards orthodoxy. Martínez de Perón was strongly influenced by José López Rega, her Minister of Social Welfare, who was considered the virtual 'prime minister' of the nation. Rega was known as *El Brujo* ('The Sorcerer') due to his passion for esotericism. The government exhibited marked administrative ineffectiveness in various areas, and violent state action against the left led to a persistent weakening of the country's political and civil liberties. Although she lacked the charisma of Eva Perón and Perón himself, her husband's death had left a general feeling of powerlessness. At first, her image as a distressed widow earned her wide political and public support, but this began to fade as the months went by, the country going into economic decline and her government dogged by controversies. Her administration proved an absolute disaster. In a year-and-a-half of calamitous management, she had six Ministers of the Interior, three Ministers of Education, four Ministers of Foreign Relations, five Ministers of Defence, six Ministers of the Economy, four Ministers of Labour and five Ministers of Social Welfare, clear evidence of the erratic course of her government.

Between 1973 and 1976, the Triple A organisation of Minister López was responsible for the disappearance and death of between 700 and 1,100 people. Given the complete inability of Isabel Perón to govern, the power was in the hands of López Rega. The Peronist *Montoneros* organisation, intending to dispute the authority of the president, announced on 6 September 1974 that it would go underground, which affected the governability of the flimsy democracy. A year later, on 8 September 1975, during Martínez de Perón's rapprochement with the military, the *Montoneros* were was declared 'illegal and terrorist' by the government.

José López Rega, Minister of Social Welfare, known as 'The Sorcerer', was the shadow behind President Isabel Perón and also the head of the infamous Triple A organisation. (Open Source)

During the rest of 1974, the terrorist organisations were very active, launching a number of major operations. Just two weeks after President Perón's death, *Montoneros* forces took over the town of General Mansilla in the province of Buenos Aires, stealing money from a local bank and weapons from the police station. On 15 July, they killed prestigious radical political leader Arturo Mor Roig in a restaurant in Ciudadela, shooting him in the back while he was having lunch with friends. Roig had been the Minister of the Interior, and his 'crime' was confronting the guerrillas using the law and justice. The following day, the ERP killed David Kraiselburd, a journalist and director of the newspaper *El Día* in the city of La

The Triple A thugs were all employees of the Ministry of Social Welfare, carrying out the dirty work of Minister López Rega (left). The emblem of Triple A (light blue outer ring with white lettering, and white central disc with gold lettering, mimicking the colours of the Argentine flag) (right) (Open Source)

The *Montoneros* murdered the radical political leader Arturo Mor Roig while he was having lunch with friends in a restaurant in Ciudadela on 15 July 1974. (*Revista Primera Plana*)

Faced with the ERP's attempt to attack the 17th Airborne Infantry Regiment, troops from the 19th Infantry Regiment were transported by helicopter to Catamarca to capture the guerrillas who had moved into the forest. Troops from the 10th and 20th Infantry Regiments also participated in the siege. (Open Source)

Plata. He had been kidnapped and kept in a 'people's jail' in the town of Gonnet but was killed by Carlos Starita when police raided the house. Starita was fatally wounded by the police during the operation. On 17 July, the ERP attacked the house of the president of the Ford Company in Argentina, using explosives to cause serious damage. Some days later, they also kidnapped for extortion the general manager of Acindar, Eric Breussi.

Meanwhile, in the forests of Tucumán, the ERP leadership was preparing its first camps for future actions in the province. The first camp was established near Ingenio Fronterita, where the ERP set up a commando comprising Mario Roberto Santucho, Manuel Negrín, Roberto Coppo, Antonio Fernández, Eduardo Pedro Palas, Salvador Falcón and Hugo Irurzún, the latter being the commander of the Mount Company. A second camp, with the same number of combatants, including some women, was established in Potrero Negro, whose commander was Leonel Juan Carlos MacDonald, known as *Comandante Raúl*. Smaller camps were set up nearby, southeast of the provincial capital, between the Lules and Salí Rivers, an area of deep, almost impenetrable forests and mountains, where it would be very difficult for government forces to locate them. The first stage of the rural guerrilla plan included the establishment of camps and the military training of their cadres, but the second stage soon started, which consisted of securing more guns, food supplies and combatants for the cause.

The Triple A organisation was also very active. On 31 July, it killed the leftist lawyer and congressman Rodolfo Ortega Peña, an important leader of the *Montoneros* who specialised in the area of political propaganda under the flag of human rights. Then on 8 August Triple A activists assassinated Horacio Chávez, Rolando Chavez and Emilio Pierini, all *Montoneros* members.

On 11 August, the ERP attempted to strike at the 17th Army Airborne Regiment in Catamarca. They intended to attack the garrison by surprise to steal their weapons, but while preparing the operation on a nearby road they were spotted and reported to the police. Police forces quickly arrived on the scene, and with the help of the military attacked the guerrillas. Finding themselves outnumbered and outgunned, the ERP team fled to their bases in the forests, leaving two dead and several wounded. At first light the next day, troops from the 19th Infantry Regiment set out from La Reducción, a town north of Famaillá, and began the ascent of Mala Mala hill in a north-westerly direction. A second column tried to block the exits to the Calchaquíes valley. The night before, a section of the 5th Arsenal Company boarded a dozen Bell UH-1H Army Aviation helicopters and moved to the top of the Mala Mala elevation to attack the supposed camp from above.

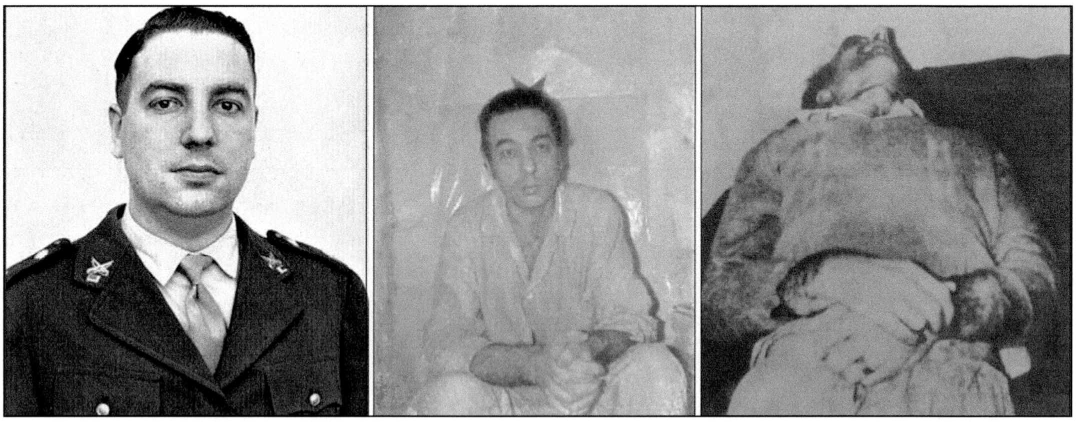

Colonel Argentino del Valle Larrabure, deputy director of the Army Gunpowder and Ammunition Factory in Villa María, Córdoba, who was kidnapped by the ERP on 12 August 1974. During his long captivity of more than a year, he was savagely tortured; he ended up being murdered by his captors in a 'people's jail' in Rosario on 19 August 1975. (CELTYV Archives)

On 16 September 1974, the ERP guerrilla Ramón Rosa Jiménez was killed in the town of Santa Lucía, in the province of Tucumán, by police forces. (Open Source)

The murder of Federal Police General Commissioner Alberto Villar (left) and his wife Elba Marina Pérez (centre) in an attack by *Montoneros* activists. On the right, the remains of the boat *Marina* in El Tigre. (CELTYV Archives)

The UH-1Hs descended into a clearing in the terrain and the troops took up positions. It was a huge pincer operation covering the El Rodeo area, with one group descending from the peaks while the other climbed the slopes, supported by heavily equipped police units wearing combat uniforms. Meanwhile, the guerrillas were constantly on the move, fleeing from both army troops and police. However, they found they were unable to leave the forest because all the routes, towns and cities in the area were controlled by army and police personnel. The siege of the guerrilla strongholds also involved an advance by the 10th Infantry Regiment and the 20th Mountain Regiment of Jujuy (reinforced by members of the Federal Police and their provincial counterparts). Part of the deployment was made in trucks, jeeps and other vehicles, with the troops armed with FAL rifles, FAP machine guns, hand grenades, flares and communications equipment, through which they maintained permanent contact with the command in Famaillá. From there, General Menéndez was able to issue directives, receive reports and evaluate the situation. The intricate terrain and thick vegetation made the advance of the troops extremely slow and difficult, but 16 guerrillas were found and killed by Army troops in the Rosary Chapel (*Capilla del Rosario*) zone, while others were captured alive. Meanwhile, Bolivia and Chile put their respective military forces on alert, redoubling surveillance and intensifying patrols along both borders, fearing that Argentine guerrillas would try to cross the passes into their countries. Despite the large military and police deployment, however, the overall results were meagre. Some people who provided logistical support were arrested, and weapons, explosives, uniforms, medical supplies and documents found in various houses that served as guerrilla hideouts were seized, but many of the insurgents escaped.

On 12 August, the ERP seized the Gunpowder and Explosives Military Factory in Villa María, Córdoba, with 100 personnel of the *Decididos de Córdoba* Company. The factory had between 60 and 70 conscript soldiers on duty, commanded by a lieutenant colonel, a major and a captain. There were also military engineers and technicians working there, together with a number of civilians. Once again, the guerrillas had an infiltrator inside the base, conscript Mario Pettiggiani. Conscript soldier José C. Fernández and Captain Roberto A. García were seriously wounded in the initial combat. Several other soldiers were wounded by the attackers, and First Corporal Marcelino Cuello was killed. There were then a series of skirmishes and a counterattack by the conscripts, forcing the withdrawal of the terrorists, leaving behind three dead and one wounded. The terrorists managed to steal 100 FAL assault rifles, 60 PAM submachine guns, four FN MAG machine guns and about 10 Madsen heavy machine guns, besides several boxes of anti-tank and

It was called the most expensive kidnapping in history. Above, from left to right, Jorge Born, Juan Born, Alberto Bosch and Juan Carlos Pérez. Below, the Born brothers during their captivity in a *Montoneros* 'people's jail'. (CELTYV Archives)

The communist politician Silvio Frondizi, brother of former president Arturo Frondizi, assassinated by the Triple A in 1974. (Open Source)

Professor Jordán Bruno Genta, a Catholic activist, was assassinated by the ERP in October 1974. (CELTYV Archives)

hand grenades and other ammunition, all of which were essential for the fighting in the Tucumán forests. Finally, they kidnapped the factory's deputy director, Army Colonel Argentino del Valle Larrabure, and Captain García. During their escape, the insurgents interrogated Captain García, who tried to flee but was severely injured and then abandoned. Colonel Larrabure suffered a long and painful captivity in a 'people's jail', only to be viciously murdered by his captors a year later. Another prisoner in the cell next door, who later escaped, reported that while ERP members were hanging Colonel Larrabure, he was singing the Argentine National Anthem.

On 22 August, the ERP attacked a police detachment using heavy weapons for the first time, with anti-tank rocket launchers and heavy machine guns. On 31 August, the FAR killed Ricardo L. Colla, executive director of the IKA Renault company at the Santa Isabel plant.

On 6 September the *Montoneros* announced their formal passage into the underground and the 'official' return of the armed struggle against the Peronist government, a mere propaganda formality since they had never abandoned terrorist actions since 1970. Just the next day, they carried out close to a dozen chain explosive attacks in Bahía Blanca, Mar del Plata, Rosario, Mendoza and Santiago del Estero. In response, the Triple A group killed the ERP defence lawyer Alfredo Curutchet in El Tigre on 13 September. On the same day, the Triple A also killed the former vice-governor of Córdoba, Hipólito Atilio López, known as *El Negro*, the union leader Juan José Varas (both sympathisers of the *Montoneros*) and Julio Troxler, former Police Deputy Chief of the province of Buenos Aires and a *Montoneros* member.

On 16 September, ERP guerrilla Ramón Rosa Jiménez (known as *Ricardo* or *El Zurdo*) was killed by police forces in Santa Lucía. In his honour, the ERP Mountain Company was named after him. Two days later, the *Montoneros* carried out an arson attack on sugar cane harvesters in Tucumán.

Army Captain Miguel Ángel Paiva, the day he got married. He was killed by the ERP on 2 October 1974 (left). Another Army officer killed by the ERP in October of that year was Major Jaime Gimeno (right). (CELTYV Archives)

Lieutenant Colonel Jorge Ibarzábal was assassinated by the ERP on 19 November 1974 after a 10-month captivity (left). His assassin was Sergio Gustavo Dicovsky (centre in the photo) (right). (Open Source)

On the following day, under the code name Operation Twins (*Operación Mellizas*), the *Montoneros* kidnapped brothers Juan and Jorge Born, both executives of the Bunge & Born Company, for ransom, killing another executive, Alberto Bosch, and his driver, Juan Carlos Pérez, in La Lucila. They requested the enormous amount of 52 million dollars for the liberation of the Born brothers, which was duly paid and both brothers were released. Then on 25 September, the ERP killed two military officers, Colonel Jorge O. Grassi in Córdoba and Lieutenant Luis R. Brize in Rosario.

A murder that shocked public opinion was carried out by the Triple A organisation, which killed communist politician Silvio Frondizi, brother of former president Arturo Frondizi, on 26 September. He was suspected of being the ideologist of the ERP, but his murder was a colossal mistake since he was not a militant and had no contact with any terrorist group. He had been a member since his youth of the Argentine Communist Party (*Partido Comunista Argentino*/PCA), which maintained an orthodox line, following directives from Moscow, and did not support the armed guerrilla fight of the 1970s.

The month of October 1974 was a violent and bloody one. On 2 October, the ERP killed Army Captain Miguel Ángel Paiva, who was shot in the back in front of his house when he was setting off for the War College, where he was a student. On the next day, the *Montoneros* killed Juan Mario Russo, former Secretary General of the Timber Guild of the province of Buenos Aires. Several days later, the ERP killed Army biochemist Major Jaime Gimeno in Banfield, but before doing so, the officer killed two of his attackers and severely wounded a third. On the 10th, the Triple A assassinated the communist militants Rodolfo Achen and Carlos Miguel, and three days later the group murdered Pedro Barraza and Carlos Laham. Also on the 10th, the ERP killed Army medical doctor Lieutenant Colonel José F. Gardón near Campo de Mayo.

On 16 October, *Montoneros* insurgents desecrated the tomb of former president Aramburu, whom they had killed in 1970, in the cemetery at Recoleta, and stole his remains. On 20 October, the ERP took over the town of Santa Lucía in Tucumán with the Mountain Company *Ramón Rosa Giménez* (*Compañía de Monte Ramón Rosa Giménez*). Three civilians were assassinated, whom it was believed were responsible for the killing of a terrorist.

The most significant killing during this time was that of Professor Jordán Bruno Genta, which occurred on the morning of 27 October. A teacher, writer, philosopher and right-wing activist, Genta was an ideologue and promoter of Catholic nationalism. That day, at 11:00 a.m., Genta left his home and went to a nearby newsstand to buy a newspaper, where a young man with a beard and wearing a brown suit shot him. The ERP claimed responsibility for the attack, arguing, among other things, that Genta had given doctrinal and spiritual advice to groups of the Triple A.

A deadly attack that shocked much of Argentina was carried out on 1 November 1974. On that date, members of the *Montoneros* assassinated the Chief of the Federal Police, General Commissioner Alberto Villar, and his wife, Elba Marina Pérez, by blowing up

The ERP terrorist Hugo Irurzún, known as *Capitán Santiago*, led the attack on the Viola family. (Open Source)

Daily tragedies were caused by the insurgents in Argentina in the 1970s. The ERP destroyed the family of Captain Humberto Viola, savagely murdering him and his 3-year-old daughter, María Cristina, seriously injuring his other daughter, 5-year-old María Fernanda. On the right, the pregnant widow of Captain Viola cries inconsolably at her husband's funeral. (CELTYV Archives)

On 28–29 September 1966, this Douglas DC-4 (registration LV-AGG) was hijacked by members of the *Movimiento Nueva Argentina* (MNA) during a flight from Buenos Aires to Río Gallegos and diverted to Port Stanley in the Falkland Islands. (Artwork by Rolando Ugolini)

BAC One-Elven 521FH registration LV-JNS was hijacked at Trelew Airport by members of the ERP, the FAR and *Montoneros* that escaped from Rawson Prison on 12 August 1972. The jet was on a flight from Comodoro Rivadavia, with stops at Trelew and Bahía Blanca, while underway to Buenos Aires. The hijackers first forced the crew to fly to Puerto Montt in Chile, and then to Santiago de Chile. (Artwork by Rolando Ugolini)

In 1973, the Argentine Air Force acquired three Sud Aviation SE 210 Caravelle VI-Ns from *Aerolineas Argentinas*. They remained in service until 1975, and were operated by Transport Group 1, 2nd Squadron of I Brigada Aérea, from El Palomar air base. During *Operativo Independencia*, they were used to transport troops to Tucumán. (Artwork by Rolando Ugolini)

Between 1967 and 1971, the Argentine Air Force acquired a total of five Fokker F.27-600 Troopships (coded T-41 to T-44) from the Netherlands. All were assigned to the 4th Squadron of I Brigada Aérea. Although experiencing a number of mishaps during their service, all were deployed intensively to transport troops around the country during the counterinsurgency operations of the 1970s. This example was delivered to Argentina in December 1971, and withdrawn from service only in 2016. (Artwork by Luca Canossa)

Starting in 1968, Argentina acquired a total of 16 Lockheed C-130 Hercules transports, including five C-130Bs, three C-130Es, five C-130Hs, two KC-130Hs and one L-100-30. All were operated by the 1st Squadron, 1st Transport Group, I Brigada Aérea, from BAM El Palomar. On 28 August 1975, the C-130E coded TC-62 was destroyed by a bomb placed on the runway at Benjamín Martinez Airport, outside Tucumán, while preparing for take-off. Out of 100 crewmembers and gendarmes on board, six were killed. Acquired in 1968, this example – code TC-63 – survived operations in support of counterinsurgency efforts and went on to serve during the Falklands/Malvinas War of 1982, when it was shot down by a Sea Harrier FRS.1. (Artwork by Tom Cooper)

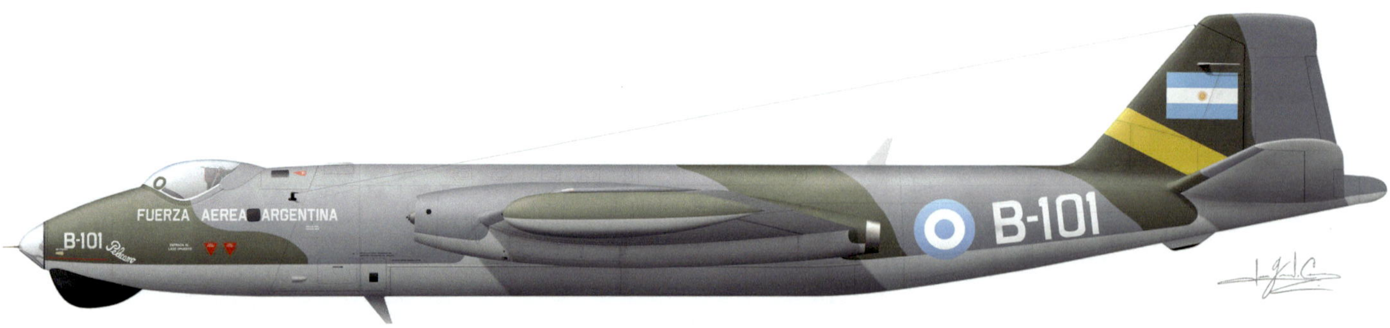

Starting in 1968, the Argentine Air Force acquired a total of 14 English Electric/BAC Canberra bombers, including 12 B.Mk 62 bombers (export variant of the B.Mk 2), and two B.Mk 64s (T.Mk 4 conversion trainers). The fleet was operated by II Brigada Aérea from BAM Paraná, in Entre Ríos province. While one (coded B-103) was destroyed in an early accident in 1971, the rest of the fleet had a colourful service. This example was one of two modified through the addition of a navigational radar installed in a black radome under the chin (the other was B-104). Some others had photoreconnaissance cameras, while standard armament included up to 2,700kg of bombs in the internal bomb bay, and up to 900kg on underwing pylons. (Artwork by Luca Canossa)

Argentina acquired a total of 100 Gloster Meteor F.Mk 4 fighters, starting in 1947. By the 1970s, the survivors were badly worn out and suffering from their intensive maintenance requirements (including engine inspections every 25 hours, and fuselage inspections every 200 hours). They kept their high-speed silver (later bare metal) overall finish for most of their career. During the last few years they were camouflaged in BS381C/638 dark sea grey and BS381C/640 dark green on upper surfaces and sides, and either BS381C/697 light admiralty grey or BS381C/172 pale roundel blue on undersides. During the 1970s, they were operated by VII Brigada Aérea. Their primary armament included four Hispano Suiza 20mm guns, and up to 16 SCAR or eight T-10 rockets could be installed under the wings. The last Argentine Meteors were withdrawn from service in 1971. (Artwork by Luca Canossa)

Starting in 1960, Argentina acquired a total of 28 North American F-86F Sabre fighters, and they were operated by the IV Brigada Aérea from BAM El Plumerilo. During overhauls at Material Area of Río Cuarto in the early 1970s at least 13 were upgraded through the installation of Collins 200B navigational systems and also received a camouflage pattern in FS3045 light tan, light blue, and FS34079 forest green on upper surfaces and sides, and FS36622 light gray on undersurfaces. In addition to six internally installed 7.62mm Browning machine guns they could be armed with two bombs of up to 250kg weight, or pods for unguided rockets. The last 10 operational F-86Fs were still active at the time of the standoff with Chile in 1978–1981 and the Falklands War of 1982. (Artwork by Tom Cooper)

Requiring a new basic trainer, in the early 1960s Buenos Aires purchased a licence for production of Beechcraft T-34A Mentor training aircraft. While 15 were acquired from the USA, 75 had been assembled locally by 1962. Initially, they served with the I Brigada Aérea from BAM Morón, but in 1970 – by when 41 had received Continental IO-470-N12B engines at the IV Material Area – the fleet was reassigned to the VII Brigada Aérea. While the majority wore a silver-grey overall finish, a few were painted in tactical camouflage and deployed for counterinsurgency operations. Such examples also received a single machine gun or camera in each wing, and underwing bomb racks and rocket rails. (Artwork by Tom Cooper)

In 1966, a total of 50 Douglas A-4B Skyhawk fighter-bombers were acquired by Argentina from surplus stocks of the US Navy. They were originally painted in silver-grey overall but in the 1970s began receiving a camouflage pattern in green and brown. All were operated by the V Brigada Aérea from BAM Coronel Pringles, outside Villa Reynolds. In addition to two internally installed Mk. 12 20mm autocannons, they were usually armed with three 250kg bombs installed on a triple ejector rack under the centreline hardpoint. (Artwork by Luca Canossa)

The Argentine Air Force acquired Dassault Mirage IIIs in two batches. The first, consisting of 10 single-seat Mirage IIIEA single-seat interceptors and two Mirage IIIDA two-seat conversion trainers received serial numbers I-003 to I-012 and I-001 to I-002, respectively. They entered service in 1972–1973 and were armed with two internally installed DEFA 30mm guns and Matra R.530F air-to-air missiles (only the second batch of seven Mirage IIIEAs arrived compatible with Matra R.550 Magic air-to-air missiles). All were operated by the VIII Brigada Aérea. (Artwork by Tom Cooper)

In response to the experience of counterinsurgency operations, in the late 1960s the Military Aircraft Factory in Córdoba developed the IA.58 Pucará light striker. First flown on 20 August 1969, the type was manufactured in a series of 98 aircraft. These were assigned to the 3rd Attack Group of the III Brigada Aérea (Reconquista), and the 4th Attack Squadron of the IX Brigada Aérea (Comodoro Rivadavia). Internal armament included four Browning 7.62mm machine guns and they could also carry up to 1,500 kilograms of bombs or rockets on underwing pylons. The first Pucará prototype – coded AX-01, as illustrated here – saw combat operations against insurgents. (Artwork by Luca Canossa)

A Morane Saulnier MS.760 Paris jet-powered trainer of the IV Brigada Aérea seen during *Operativo Independencia* in 1975. Notable is the tactical camouflage pattern applied for counterinsurgency operations. (via SOP (ret.) Walter Bentancor)

An A-4B (serial number C-207) of the V Brigada Aérea, seen in the mid-1970s. (via Vladimiro Cettolo)

An A-4C Skyhawk (serial C-319), waiting for the next training sortie. Notable under the intake is one of two Colt Mk. 12 20mm guns. (via Vladimiro Cettolo)

During the mid-1970s the Argentine Air Force still had a total of 14 Douglas C-47 Dakota transports in operational service. This example was coded TC-21. (Photo by Horacio Gareiso)

Two helicopter types used by the Naval Aviation Command (COAN) in the mid-1970s: upper photograph shows a Sikorsky S-61D-4 (serial 2-H-231), while the lower one shows an Aerospatiale SA.316B Alouette III (serial 4-H-23). (Amilarg)

(Map by Antonio Luis Sapienza)

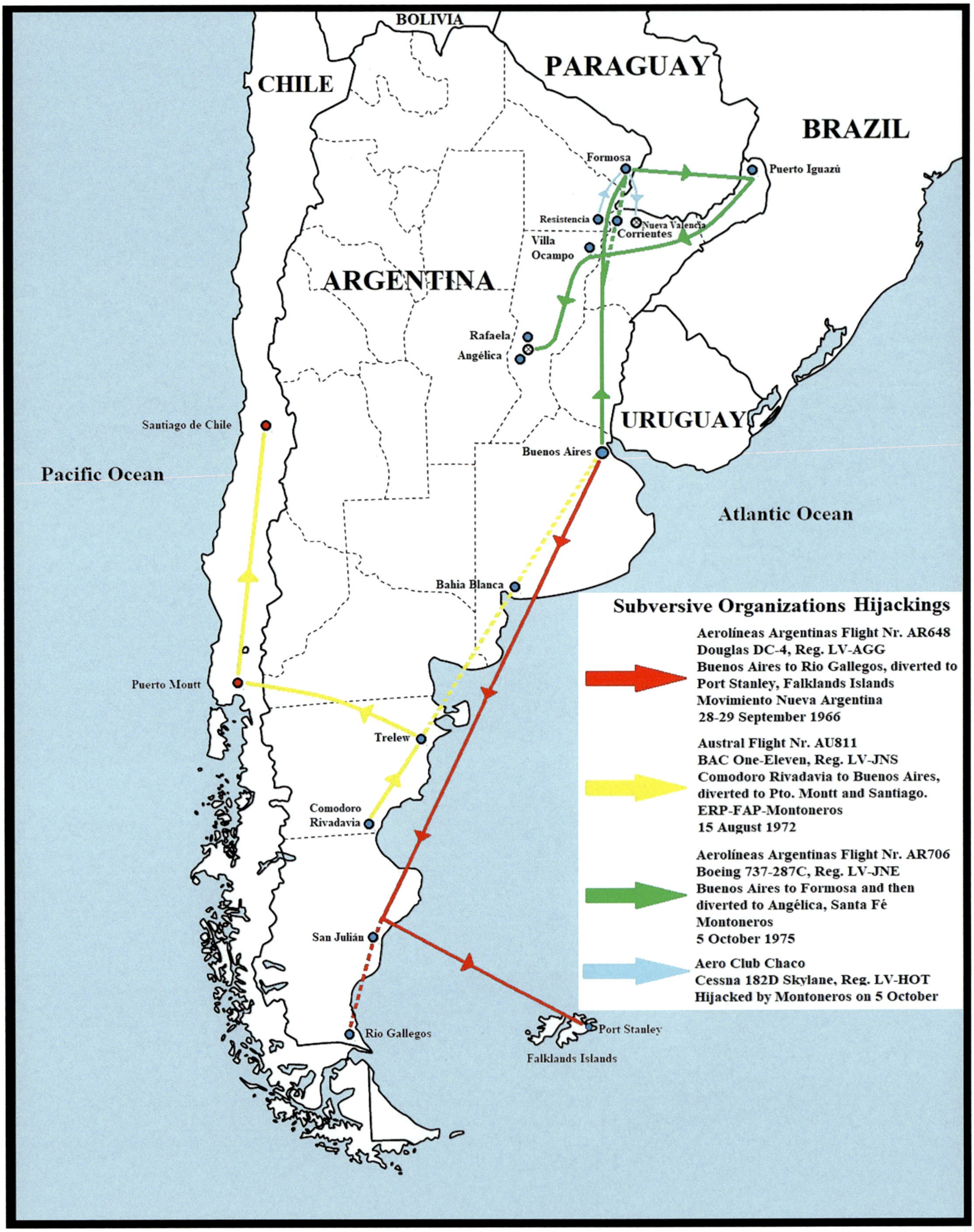

(Map by Antonio Luis Sapienza)

his boat, the *Marina*, while sailing on Rosquete Creek in El Tigre. Commissioner Villar took regular trips in the area in his pleasure boat, always accompanied by his wife. The previous night, two ERP divers had placed 20 kilograms of trotyl on Villar's boat under the driver's seat. The explosives were then activated by remote control.

At this time, the subversive gangs also threatened to attack primary and secondary schools. The announcement tended to generate panic and increase the climate of uncertainty in the country. The first sign that the insurgents were serious took place on Monday, 4 November, when two students, aged just 8 and 9, were kidnapped in the federal capital and Ciudadela while on their way to school. The children were picked up from public roads by several strangers and kept captive in remote places. When they were released, they were told not to go to their homes but to their schools and to tell the authorities there to close them until further notice. In view of this, the government adopted measures in cooperation with the Army, the Navy, the Air Force and the respective national and provincial police forces in order to protect the students. The measures were put in force in the federal capital and the surrounding areas of Greater Buenos Aires.

Army troops from different regiments were deployed in Tucumán throughout 1974, setting up control points on highways and in cities and carrying out the first incursions into the forests of the province. (*Ejército Argentino*)

Meanwhile, the ERP continued killing Army officers. On 7 November, they assassinated Army Major Néstor Horacio López in Santa Fé, then Army First Lieutenant Antonio Eduardo Carbajo in San Nicolás on the 12th and Army Lieutenant Colonel Jorge Ibarzábal, who had been kidnapped 10 months earlier in Azul, on the 19th. Ibarzábal was being transported in a van when the police intercepted them, but the rebels managed to kill him before he could be freed. The assassin was Sergio Gustavo Dicovsky, an ERP terrorist who was an architecture student at the University of Buenos Aires; he was shot a few days later by the police. The inhumane treatment to which Lieutenant Colonel Ibarzábal was subjected during his captivity caused a loss of body weight of 30 kilograms (66lb). Promoted *post-mortem* to colonel, he was 46 years old when he was assassinated.

On 22 November, the *Montoneros* machinegunned the façade and windows of the building of the Navy Electronics Directorate on Malabia Street in Palermo, Buenos Aires. This attack was carried out by Rodolfo Walsh (known as *Esteban*), Paco Urondo (*Ítalo*), Horacio Verbitsky (*Roberto*) and Norberto Habbeger.

In December 1974, the ERP killed Army Captain Humberto Viola and his 3-year-old daughter. Another daughter, aged 5, was severely wounded and his pregnant wife, Maby Picón, miraculously survived unscathed. All members of the family were in a car going to a family event when they were intercepted by ERP terrorists who opened fire indiscriminately, regardless of the presence of the little girls and the pregnant wife. When the shooting began, a wounded Captain Viola ran out of the car so that the attackers would stop shooting at his family and was immediately gunned down. The murders were committed by an ERP commando group led by Hugo Irurzún (known as *Santiago*), who would be caught and killed by the Paraguayan police after the assassination of former Nicaraguan president Anastasio Somoza in 1980 in Asunción. Terrorist actions like these turned the general population against the rebels, who never enjoyed popular support, one of the reasons for their resounding failure. Just three days later, the ERP continued their deadly campaign when they assassinated Ramón Samaniego, executive director of the La Cantábrica company.

The Triple A organisation responded with several murders in December 1974, assassinating the *Montonero* militant Roberto Silvestre, the leftist professor Enrique Rusconi and leftist leaders María Baldi, Héctor Cois, J. Luces, A. Celina, R. Valverde, L. Cuiña and Juan Alberto Campos.

During the second semester of 1974, the actions in Tucumán gained greater importance, the presence of the guerrillas was consolidated and the conflict as a whole acquired the nature of war. Indeed, although not declared, there was open warfare, with the constant movement of troops, the presence of camps, clashes in rural areas and attacks in urban centres. The situation became much more dangerous after the fighting in Catamarca. The defeated rebels sought to return to their centres of operations in the mountains and the leadership mobilised new cadres to reinforce their weak situation.

It is widely believed that the armed forces began operations only after the signing of Decree 261/75 by the constitutional government, but that was not the case. Throughout 1974, especially in the second half of the year, the Army, the Federal and Provincial Police and the Gendarmerie manoeuvred their units and began preparations to neutralise the enemy and reduce their power, both in terms of fire and movement. By order of the Army Commander-in-Chief, the 19th Infantry Regiment, 5th Mountain Communications Company and 5th Arsenal Company *Miguel de Azcuénaga* were mobilised, being part of the Army's V Infantry Brigade based in

Tucumán. Only hours later, similar orders were issued for the 28th Mountain Infantry Regiment of Tartagal (*Regimiento de Infantería de Montaña* 28/RIM 28) and 5th Mountain Artillery Group, part of the 20th Mountain Infantry Regiment (RIM 20), whose base was in Jujuy. These units had to manoeuvre on the backs of mules, which provided the best way for them to move over rugged terrain such as that around Aconquija.

The violent incursions of the guerrilla forces in different areas of Argentina, especially the attacks on military units, had received a negative response among the general population, with many calling for a tougher government reaction, including military intervention.

In light of the demands for more action, there were several appointments and promotions in the armed forces throughout December 1974. The most important of these in the Argentine Army were as shown in Table 1.[1]

As for the Argentine Air Force, the following officers were promoted to brigadier: Roberto Temporini, Aldo Mario Barbuy, Norberto Sciutto and Raúl Iván Yansen, all commodores of the air rank. Commodores of the general ranks also promoted to brigadier were Juan Tomás Cubría and Rubén Luis Bonoris, along with from the technical ranks Leopoldo Gallo and César Ferrante.

Many senior Argentine Navy officers were also promoted as shown in Table 2.[2]

On 14 December, the police discovered a house in Lomas de Zamora where a 'people's jail' was operating. During an intense firefight, two guerrillas and one policeman were killed, with several others on both sides wounded.

On 22 December, the ERP killed 41-year-old Dr Carlos Alberto Sacheri, a philosopher and professor at the University of Buenos Aires, Salvador University and the Argentine Catholic University.

Table 1: Army Appointments in December 1974

Officer	Unit
Major General Alberto Numa Laplane	Commander of the I Army Corps
Brigadier General Guillermo Ramón Ezcurra	Deputy Commander of the I Army Corps
Major General Luis Carlos Gómez Centurión	Commander of the II Army Corps
Brigadier General Leopoldo Fortunato Galtieri	Deputy Commander of the II Army Corps
Major General Enrique E. Salgado	Commander of the III Army Corps
Brigadier General Rodolfo Cánepa	Deputy Commander of the III Army Corps
Brigadier General Eduardo José Ignacio Betti	Commander of the V Army Corps
Brigadier General Genaro Ramón Díaz Bessone	Deputy Commander of the V Army Corps
Brigadier General Carlos C.I. Delía Azpitarte	Director of the Military Institutes
Major General Ernesto Della Croce	Commander of the Joint Chiefs of Staff
Brigadier General Jorge Rafael Videla	Commander of the General Staff
Brigadier General Luciano Benjamín Menéndez	Chief of Staff
Brigadier General Guillermo Suárez Mason	Head of the Army Intelligence
Brigadier General Francisco Rosas Méndez	Head of the Army Operations
Brigadier General José Montes	Head of the Army Logistics
Brigadier General Antonio D. Bussi	Head of the Army Finance
Brigadier General Roberto Eduardo Viola	Head of the General Command Secretariat
Brigadier General Alberto Samuel Cáceres	Commander of the National Gendarmerie
Brigadier General José Antonio Vaquero	Director of the Military School
Brigadier General Carlos Ladislaw	Director of the Army War School
Brigadier General Albano Harguindeguy	Commander of the 1st Armoured Cavalry Regiment (Tandil)
Brigadier General Luciano A. Jáuregui	Commander of the 2nd Armoured Cavalry Regiment (Paraná)
Brigadier General José T. Goyret	Commander of the 3rd Infantry Regiment (Curuzú Cuatiá)
Brigadier General Rodolfo C. Mujica	Commander of the 4th Airborne Infantry Regiment (Córdoba)
Brigadier General Ricardo A. Muñoz	Commander of the 5th Infantry Regiment (Tucumán)
Brigadier General Juan A Buasso	Commander of the 6th Infantry Regiment (Neuquén)
Brigadier General Carlos Dalla Tea	Commander of the 7th Infantry Regiment (Corrientes)
Brigadier General Fernando Santiago	Commander of the 8th Mount Infantry Regiment (Mendoza)
Brigadier General Adolfo Sigwald	Commander of the 9th Infantry Regiment (Comodoro Rivadavia)
Brigadier General Otto Paladino	Commander of the 10th Infantry Regiment (Buenos Aires)

Table 2: Naval officer promotions	
Officer	**Unit**
Rear Admiral Luis Alberto Mendía	Commander of Naval Operations
Rear Admiral Horacio González Llanos	Naval Operations Chief of Staff
Rear Admiral Cesáreo Goñi	Commander of the Naval Aviation
Rear Admiral Julio Juan Bardi	Commander of the Marine Infantry Corps
Rear Admiral Luis Casanova	Director of the Navy War School
Rear Admiral Julio A. Torti	Deputy Director of the National Defence School
Navy Captain Horacio Justo Gómez Beret	Chief of Staff Operations
Navy Captain Manuel Jacinto García	Commander of the Navy Prefecture (Coast Guard)
Navy Captain Edgardo José Segura	Commander of the South Naval Area
Navy Captain Eduardo René Fracassi	Naval General Secretary
Navy Captain Lorenzo de Mantmollín	Chief of Staff Intelligence Chief
Navy Captain Norberto C. Bonesana	Director of Naval Justice
Navy Captain Aldo De Rosso	Director of Naval Weaponry
Navy Captain Humberto J. Barbuzzi	Commander of the ARA *25 de Mayo* aircraft carrier
Navy Captain Luis P. Sánchez Moreno	Commander of the Destroyers' First Division
Navy Captain Pedro A. Santamaría	Commander of the Destroyers' Second Division
Navy Captain Edmundo O. Núñez	Commander of the ARA *General Belgrano* light cruiser
Navy Captain José E. Cortinés	Commander of the Submarine Force
Navy Captain Fernando Miguel Romero	Commander of the Antarctica Naval Group

Another university professor and Catholic activist, Carlos Alberto Sacheri, was assassinated by the ERP in December 1974. He is shown with his wife and their six children. (*Periódico católico La Esperanza*)

Deeply Catholic, he had published several books denouncing the Marxist incursion into the Catholic Church through the Movement of Priests for the Third World, who protected and counselled subversive groups. That day, after leaving mass, he was returning home in his car with his wife and seven children when he was assassinated in front of his family. The following day, the car of General Commissioner Luis Margaride and his escort was attacked. Insurgents detonated a bomb planted in a pick-up truck parked on the street, resulting in injuries to several police officers. ERP guerrilla snipers fired upon the police from a building under construction, but the officers managed to call for reinforcements, who arrived quickly and the guerrillas fled. The ERP had targeted Commissioner Margaride because they linked him to the murders carried out by the Triple A.

Between May 1969 and December 1974, a staggering 1,386 acts of a terrorist nature took place in Argentina: 384 sabotages and attacks, 254 takeovers of towns and facilities, 86 robberies, 50 kidnappings for extortion, 541 murders and 71 terrorist escapes.

The objective of all the guerrilla organisations in Argentina was to convince the proletarian masses of the worthiness of their objectives, but in this they patently did not succeed. The common people did not want anything to do with the guerrillas, on many occasions refusing their offers of money, toys for poor children, medical assistance and various gifts. The public often called the police, Gendarmerie or the Army to denounce the insurgents and openly cooperated with the government's forces of law and order. This was a decisive factor in the military defeat of the guerrillas.

3
THE ARGENTINE ARMED FORCES IN THE MID-1970S

Fuerza Aérea Argentina (Argentine Air Force)

In the 1970s, the the commanders of the Argentine Air Force were as shown in Table 3.[1]

Table 3: Commanders of the Air Force in the 1970s	
Officer	**Term**
Brigadier General Carlos Rey	12 March 1970 to 25 May 1973
Brigadier General Héctor Fautario	25 May 1973 to 18 December 1975
Brigadier General Orlando Agosti	18 December 75 to 25 January 1979

Commanders of the Argentine Air Force in the 1970s. From left to right, Brigadier General Carlos Rey, Brigadier General Héctor Fautario and Brigadier General Orlando Agosti. (*Fuerza Aérea Argentina*)

President María Estela Martínez de Perón with the Commander of the Air Force, Brigadier General Héctor Fautario, and other high-ranking officers during the celebration of the Air Force anniversary on 10 August 1974 at El Palomar Air Force Base. (*Revista Aeroespacio*)

Argentine Air Force Lockheed C-130E Hercules serial TC-63 in the 1970s. This C-130 was shot down on 1 June 1982 by the Royal Navy Sea Harrier serial XZ451 during the Falklands War. (Jorge Lonardi)

Argentine Air Force Sud Aviation SE 210 Caravelle VI-N serial T-93 in 1972. (Atilio Marino)

Boeing 707-3F3B serial T-01 (later TC-91), baptised with the name *Soberanía* (Sovereignty), purchased new from the factory in 1975 (left). Fokker F.28 Mk.1000M serial T-02, baptised as *Patagonia,* acquired in 1970 (original serial T-01). Both were from I Air Brigade of the Air Force. (*Dirección de Estudios Históricos de la Fuerza Aérea Argentina*)

Air Force Fokker F.27 Mk.400M serial TC-73. (Via Vladimiro Cettolo)

II Air Brigade BAC Canberra B.Mk.62 serial B-105. (*Amilarg*)

Two III Air Brigade FMA IA.58 Pucarás, serials A-505 and AX-03, flying in formation in the mid-1970s. (Via Vladimiro Cettolo)

The Argentine Air Force was organised as shown in Table 4.[2]

Table 4: Argentine Air Force Air Brigades

Air Brigade	Location	Base	Groups	Aircraft
I	El Palomar	BAM El Palomar	1st Transport Group	
			1st Squadron	C-130E/H Hercules
			2nd Squadron	SE 210 Caravelle VI-N, Fokker F.28
			3rd Squadron	C-47, IA.50 Guaraní II, Aero Commander 500
			4th Squadron	Fokker F.27
			5th Squadron	Boeing 707-3F3B
			1st & 2nd Observation Group	Piper J-3 Cub
			Base Group Nr. 1	
			Technical Group Nr. 1	
II	Paraná	BAM General Urquiza	1st Bombardment Squadron – 2nd Bombardment Group	B.Mk.62/T.Mk.64 Canberra
			2nd Transport Group	Douglas C-47, Fokker F.27, Aero Commander AC500
			1st Photographic Group	IA.50 Guaraní II, Learjet 35A, IA.35 Huanquero, Hughes 369HS.
			Base Group Nr. 2	
			Technical Group Nr. 2	

Table 4: Argentine Air Force Air Brigades (*continued*)

III	Reconquista	BAM Reconquista	3rd Attack Group	FMA IA.58 Pucará
			Base Group Nr. 3	
			Technical Group Nr. 3	
IV	Mendoza	BAM El Plumerillo	1st Fighter-Bomber Group (CB-1)	F-86F Sabre
			2nd Fighter-Bomber Group (CB-2)	MS.760 Paris
			3rd Fighter-Bomber Group (CB-3)	MS.760 Paris
			4th Fighter Group (C-4)	A-4C Skyhawk
			SAR	SA315B Lama, Hughes 369HS, Cessna 182
			Base Group Nr. 4	
			Technical Group Nr. 4	
V	Villa Reynolds	BAM Coronel Pringles	5th Fighter Group (C-5)	A-4B/C Skyhawk
			Base Group Nr. 5	
			Technical Group Nr. 5	
VI	Tandil	BAM Tandil	SAR	HU-16/SA-16A/B Albatross
			Anti-Aircraft Artillery Group 1	
			Base Group Nr. 6	
			Technical Group Nr. 6	
VII	Morón	BAM Morón	7th Air Group	
			1st Helicopter Squadron	Bell UH-1D/H
			2nd Helicopter Squadron	Hughes 369, Hughes 500C/D/E
			3rd Helicopter Squadron	Sikorsky S61N/R
			4th Helicopter Squadron	Sikorsky S58DT
			5th Helicopter Squadron	SA315B Lama, Hiller SL4
			Base Group Nr. 7	
			Technical Group Nr. 7	
VIII	Mariano Moreno	BAM Mariano Moreno	8th Fighter Group (C-8)	Dassault Mirage IIIEA/DA
			Base Group Nr. 8	
			Technical Group Nr. 8	
IX	Comodoro Rivadavia	BAM Comodoro Rivadavia	9th Air Transport Group	Fokker F.27, Fokker F.28, DHC-6 Twin Otter, Aero Commander 500
			Base Group Nr. 9	
			Technical Group Nr. 9	
Military Aviation School	Córdoba	Córdoba	Training Air Groups	Beechcraft B-45 Mentor, Morane-Saulnier MS.760 Paris
INAC	Morón	BAM Morón	Civil Aviation Personnel Training	Max Holste MH.1521 Broussard, Aero Commander 500, Cessna 180A, IA.51 Tehuelche, Cessna FMA A-182, IA.50 Guaraní II, Cessna 320, Hughes 369/500, Aero Boero 180, Piper PA-31P Navajo, Cessna 210B Centurion, Cessna 336 Skymaster
COA	Buenos Aires	Condor Building	Air Operations Command	Rockwell 75A Sabreliner
LADE	El Palomar	BAM El Palomar	Airline run by the Air Force	Fokker F.27, Fokker F.28, DHC-6 Twin Otter

IV Air Brigade North American F-86F Sabre serial C-120. (Jorge Lonardi)

VI Air Brigade Grumman SA-16A Albatross serial BS-3. (Jorge Lonardi)

Some helicopter types of the VII Air Brigade. Clockwise, Bell UH-1D, Hughes 369, Sikorsky S-61N and Sikorsky S.58T. (*Amilarg*, Dick Lohuis)

VIII Air Brigade Dassault Mirage IIIEA serial I-007 (left). (Via SOP (Ret) Walter Bentancor).
A pair of Mirage IIIEAs about to take-off (right). (Carlos Ay)

IX Air Brigade De Havilland Canada DHC-6-200 Twin Otter serial T-81 (left). (Martín Kubo)
I Air Brigade FMA IA.50 Guaraní serial T-116 (right). (Via Vladimiro Cettolo)

Military Aviation School trainers, a Beechcraft B-45/T-34A Mentor (left) and
Morane-Saulnier MS.760 Paris (right). (*Amilarg*, Javier Mosquera)

Table 5: Argentine Air Force aircraft on strength in the mid-1970s[3]		
Type/Years in service	**Number of aircraft**	**Role**
Dassault Mirage IIIEA/DA (1972–2015)	9/2	Supersonic fighter-interceptor
Douglas A-4B (A-4P) Skyhawk (1966–1999)	36	Attack
Douglas A-4C Skyhawk (1975–1999)	21	Attack
North American F-86F-30 Sabre (1960–1986)	13	Jet fighter-bomber
BAC Mk.62/T.Mk.64 Canberra (1970–2000)	9/2	Tactical bomber
FMA IA.58 Pucará (1975–2019)	17	Attack/close air support
Morane-Saulnier MS.760 Paris (1958–2006)	36	Advanced trainer/light attack
Beechcraft B-45 (T-34A) Mentor (1957–2011)	51	Primary trainer
Sud Aviation SE 210 VI-N Caravelle (1973–1975)	3	Passenger transport
Boeing 707-387B (1975–2008)	1	Passenger Transport
Fokker F.28 Mk.1000/4000 Fellowship (1975–2020)	7	Passenger transport
Lockheed C-130E/H Hercules (1968–present)	2/5	Heavy cargo & troop transport/aerial refuelling
Fokker F.27 Mk.400M Troopship/Mk.600 Friendship (1968–2016)	11	Passenger/troop transport
Douglas DC-3/C-47 (1943–1990)	14	Transport
Grumman UH-16B/SA-16A Albatross (1952–1979)	2	Transport/SAR

Table 5: Argentine Air Force aircraft on strength in the mid-1970s[3] *(continued)*		
FMA IA.50 Guaraní II (1966–2007)	35	Transport
De Havilland DHC-3 Otter (1966–1973)	3	Transport
De Havilland DHC-6-200 Twin Otter (1968–present)	6	Transport
Rockwell 75A Sabreliner (1974–2005)	1	VIP Transport
Max Holste MH.1521 Broussard (1958–1990)	10	Light transport
Aero Commander 500 U/B (1968–2005)	16	Light transport
Piper PA-31P-325 Navajo (1973–present)	3	Light transport
Cessna 170B (1958–1980)	1	Light transport
Cessna/FMA A-182J/K/L/N (1966–present)	39	Light transport/liaison
Cessna U.17A Skywagon (1967–present)	10	Light transport/liaison
Cessna 210B Centurion (1974–1986)	1	Light transport
Cessna 310 (1974–present)	2	Light transport
Cessna 320 Skyknight (1968–1982)	1	Light transport
Cessna 336 Skymaster (1974–1978)	1	Light transport
Piper J-3 Cub / PA-12 (1946–1980)	5	Liaison
FMA IA-46 Ranquel (1957–present)	18	Liaison/tug plane
FMA IA.51 Tehuelche (1963–1981)	1	Tug plane
Aero Boero 180RVR (1973–present)	3	Liaison
Bell 47G.2A (1969–1977)	3	Multipurpose helicopter
Sikorsky S-61N/S-61R Pelican (1975–2002)	1/1	SAR
Bell UH-1D/H (1967–present)	12	Multipurpose helicopter
Hiller SL4 (1967–1977)	3	Multipurpose helicopter
Hughes 369 HM/HS/HE (1969–2008)	14	Observation/light attack/ close air support helicopter
Hughes 500C/D/E (1976–present)	18	Multipurpose/light attack/ close air support
Aerospatiale SA315B Lama (1973–present)	12	Utility helicopter
Sikorsky S-58DT (1975–1980)	2	Utility helicopter

Armada Argentina (Argentine Navy/ARA)

In the 1970s, the commanders of the Navy were as shown in Table 6.[4]

Table 6: Commanders of the Navy in the 1970s	
Officer	**Term**
Admiral Carlos Coda	03 January 1972 to 25 May 1973
Admiral Carlos Álvarez	25 May 1973 to 06 December 1973
Admiral Emilio Massera	06 December 1973 to 15 September 1978
Admiral Armando Lambruschini	15 September 1978 to 11 September 1981

The Argentine Navy Commanders in the 1970s. From left to right, Admiral Carlos Coda, Admiral Carlos Álvarez, Admiral Emilio Massera and Admiral Armando Lambruschini. (Armada Argentina)

The Commander of the Argentine Navy, Admiral Emilio Massera, with President Isabel Perón during the Navy anniversary at Puerto Belgrano Naval Base on 5 May 1975. (*Archivo General de la Nación*)

Argentine Navy vessels. Clockwise, aircraft carrier ARA *25 de Mayo*, light cruiser ARA *General Belgrano*, submarine ARA *Salta* and destroyer ARA *Espora*. (Histarmar Archives)

More Argentine Navy vessels. Clockwise, patrol boat ARA *Murature*, minesweeper ARA *Rio Negro*, transport ship ARA *Bahía Aguirre* and PT boat ARA *Intrépida*. (Histarmar Archives)

In the mid-1970s, the Argentine Navy was one of the most powerful navies in Latin America, with one aircraft carrier, three light cruisers, nine destroyers, four submarines, two patrol boats, six minesweepers, five PT boats, five transport ships, one training frigate, four hydrographic ships, one oceanographic boat, one LSD (landing ship, dock), seven LCILs (landing craft infantry, large), four LSTs (landing ship, tank), nine ocean tugs, six tugs, three yachts (one presidential among them), three gasoline tankers and a floating dock. Details are shown in Table 7.

Table 7: Argentine Navy ships on strength in the 1970s

Type (Class)	Pennant Number	Name	Tons	Crew
Aircraft Carrier (Colossus)	V-2	ARA *25 de Mayo*	19,720	1,200
Light Cruiser (-)	C-3	ARA *La Argentina*	8,632	800
Light Cruiser (Brooklyn)	C-4	ARA *General Belgrano*	12,650	975–1,100
Light Cruiser (Brooklyn)	C-5	ARA *Nueve de Julio*	13,430	1,100
Destroyer (Type 42)	D-1	ARA *Hércules*	4,075	300
Destroyer (Type 42) (*)	D-2	ARA *Santímisa Trinidad*	4,820	287
Destroyer (Fletcher)	D-20	ARA *Brown*	3,030	250
Destroyer (Fletcher)	D-21	ARA *Espora*	3,030	250
Destroyer (Fletcher)	D-22	ARA *Rosales*	3.892	200
Destroyer (Fletcher)	D-23	ARA *Almirante Domecq García*	3,048	230
Destroyer (Fletcher)	D-24	ARA *Almirante Storni*	3,048	230
Destroyer (Sumner)	D-25	ARA *Segui*	3,311	180
Destroyer (Sumner)	D-26	ARA *Bouchard*	3,225	180
Destroyer (Gearing)	D-27	ARA *Py*	3,532	200
Submarine (Balao/Guppy II)	S-21	ARA *Santa Fe*	1,870	76–78
Submarine (Balao/Guppy II)	S-22	ARA *Santiago del Estero*	2,425	85
Submarine (209-1200)	S-31	ARA *Salta*	1,285	36
Submarine (209-1200)	S-32	ARA *San Luís*	1,285	36
Patrol Boat (Murature)	P-20	ARA *Murature*	1,100	130
Patrol Boat (Murature)	P-21	ARA *King*	1,100	130
Minesweeper (Ton)	M-1	ARA *Neuquén*	425	32
Minesweeper (Ton)	M-2	ARA *Rio Negro*	425	32

Table 7: Argentine Navy ships on strength in the 1970s *(continued)*

Minesweeper (Ton)	M-3	ARA *Chubut*	425	32
Minesweeper (Ton)	M-4	ARA *Tierra del Fuego*	425	32
Minesweeper (Ton)	M-5	ARA *Chaco*	425	32
Minesweeper (Ton)	M-6	ARA *Formosa*	425	32
PT Boat (Zurubí)	P-55	ARA *Zurubí*	65	4/5
PT Boat (Higgins)	P-82	ARA LT3/*Alakush*	52	15
PT Boat (Higgins)	P-84	ARA LT5/*Towora*	52	15
PT Boat (Lürssen TNC-45)	P-85	ARA *Intrépida*	268	39
PT Boat (Lürssen TNC-45)	P-86	ARA *Indómita*	268	39
Transport Ship (-)	B-2	ARA *Bahía Aguirre*	5,308	100
Transport Ship (-)	B-6	ARA *Bahía Buen Suceso*	5,305	100
Transport Ship (FS)	B-7	ARA *San Julián*	953	40
Transport Ship (-)	B-8	ARA *Bahía Thetis*	5,225	46
Training Ship (-)	Q-76	ARA *Capitán Brizuela*	1,100	25
Training Frigate (-)	Q-2	ARA *Libertad*	18,500	110
Hydrographic Boat (-)	Q-10	ARA *Ushuaia*	1,275	65
Hydrographic Boat	Q-11	ARA *Comodoro Rivadavia*	827	36
Hydrographic Boat (-)	Q-15	ARA *Cormorán*	99	21
Hydrographic Boat (-)	Q-16	ARA *Petrel*	54	8
Rescue Boat	Q-18	ARA *Guardiamarina Zicari*	1,750	80
Hydrographic Boat (Sotoyomo)	RHF2/A-8	ARA *Sanaviron*	800	50
Hydrographic Boat (Eltanin)	-	ARA *Islas Orcadas*	3,750	38–48
Oceanographic Boat (-)	Q-47	ARA *El Austral*	565	25
LSD (Ashland)	Q-43	ARA *Cándido de Lasala*	9,375	250
LCIL (LCI 351)	Q-54	ARA *BDI-1*	380	20–25
LCIL (LCI 351)	Q-55	ARA *BDI-2*	380	20–25
LCIL (LCI 351)	Q-56	ARA *BDI-3*	380	20–25
LCIL (LCI 351)	Q-57	ARA *BDI-4*	380	20–25
LCIL (LCI 351)	Q-58	ARA *BDI-5*	380	20–25
LCIL (LCI 351)	Q-59	ARA *BDI-6*	380	20–25
LCIL (LCI 351)	Q-60	ARA *BDI-7*	380	20–25
LST (LST 542) and 2 LCVPs	Q-44/BDT-4	ARA *Cabo San Gonzalo*	8,000	50
LST (LST 542) and 2 LCVPs	Q-46/BDT-6	ARA *Cabo San Isidro*	8,000	50
LST (LST 542) and 2 LCVPs	Q-50/BDT-10	ARA *Cabo San Pío*	8,000	50
LST (LST 1171)	Q-42	ARA *Cabo San Antonio*	8,000	124
Ocean Tug (Abnaki)	A-1	ARA *Comandante Gral. Yrigoyen*	1,850	85
Ocean Tug (Abnaki)	A-2	ARA *Comandante General Zapiola*	1,675	80
Ocean Tug (Abnaki)	A-3	ARA *Francisco de Gurruchaga*	1,780	75
Ocean Tug (V-4)	A-4	ARA *Thompson*	1,863	60
Ocean Tug (AT)	A-5	ARA *Diaguita*	814	50
Ocean Tug (AT)	A-6	ARA *Yamana*	800	50
Ocean Tug (AT)	A-7	ARA *Chiriguano*	800	50
Ocean Tug (Sotoyomo)	A-9	ARA *Alférez Sobral*	848	49
Ocean Tug (Sotoyomo)	A-10	ARA *Comodoro Somellera*	848	49
Tug (YTL)	R-6	ARA *Calchaqui*	75	5
Tug (-)	R-7	ARA *Toba*	340	35
Tug (YTL)	R-16	ARA *Capayan*	69	5

Table 7: Argentine Navy ships on strength in the 1970s *(continued)*				
Tug (-)	R-29	ARA *Pehuenche*	330	14
Tug (-)	R-30	ARA *Tonocote*	330	14
Tug (-)	R-32	ARA *Quilmes*	355	14
Presidential Yacht (-)	Q-72	ARA *Tecuara*	295	10
Yacht (-)	Q-74	ARA *Fortuna*	32	6
Yacht (-)	Q-75	ARA *Fortuna II*	17	3
Gasoline Tanker (T1-M-BT1)	B-16	ARA *Punta Delgada*	6,187	90
Gasoline Tanker (-)	B-18	ARA *Punta Médanos*	16,300	140
Gasoline Tanker (-)	B-21	ARA *Punta Alta*	1,900	40
Floating Dock (ARD-12)	Y-1	-	3,500	31
(*) launched in 1974 but after the 1975 terrorist attack, its delivery to the Navy was delayed until 1980.				

The Argentine Navy had its main base in Puerto Belgrano, near Bahía Blanca, a smaller base in Río Santiago, which was the garrison of the Naval School and the Naval Lyceum, the submarine naval base of Mar del Plata, Zárate Naval Base and the naval base in Ushuaia. In the federal capital, there was the Navy Mechanics School (ESMA/ *Escuela de Mecánica de la Armada*).

The Argentine Navy was organised into three naval zones:

- The Fluvial Naval Zone, including the provinces of Misiones, Corrientes, Chaco, Formosa, Santa Fé, Entre Ríos and Buenos Aires. Headquarters: Zárate Naval Base.
- The Atlantic Naval Zone, including the area from Cabo San Antonio in the province of Buenos Aires to the city of Comodoro Rivadavia in the province of Chubut. Headquarters: Mar del Plata Naval Base.
- The Austral Naval Zone, including the provinces of Santa Cruz and Tierra del Fuego, the Fuegian channels and Argentine Antarctica. Headquarters: Ushuaia Naval Base.

Naval Aviation Command (*Comando de la Aviación Naval Argentina*/COAN)

In 1972, the Naval Aviation received 16 Douglas A-4Q Skyhawks to be used on board the ARA *25 de Mayo* aircraft carrier and on land naval bases, which replaced the ageing Grumman F9F-2 Panther fighters. Regarding transport aircraft, Lockheed L-188 Electras and Pilatus PC-6B Turbo Porters were incorporated. Sikorsky S-61 Sea King helicopters were also purchased in the 1970s. Some older types like the Lockheed P.2 Neptune, Grumman S2A Tracker, Douglas C-47, North American T-28 Fennec and Aerospatiale SA.316B Alouette III continued on active service throughout the 1970s, as did the Aermacchi MB.326GB advanced trainer/light attack jets. The Naval Aviation was organised into six naval air squads, as outlined in Table 8.[5]

Table 8: Argentine Naval Aviation Squadrons	
Air Naval Squadron	**Air Naval Groups**
1st	Naval Aviation School (ESAN) 2nd Air Naval General Purpose Squadron 2nd Air Naval Attack Squadron 4th Air Naval Fighter and Attack Squadron
2nd	Air Naval Anti-Submarine Squadron 2nd Air Naval Transport Squadron
3rd	2nd Air Naval Transport Squadron 3rd Air Naval Fighter and Attack Squadron 1st Air Naval Helicopter Squadron 2nd Air Naval Helicopter Squadron
4th	4th Air Naval Fighter and Attack Squadron Air Naval Reconnaissance Squadron
5th	1st & 2nd Air Naval Mobile Logistics Support Squadrons
6th	2nd Air Naval General Purpose Squadron

Table 9: Argentine Naval Aviation aircraft types on strength in the mid-1970s[6]		
Type/Years in service	**Number of aircraft**	**Role**
Douglas A-4Q Skyhawk (1972–1988)	11	Fighter/attack
Aermacchi MB.326GB Pelican (1968–2007)	8	Advanced jet trainer/attack
Grumman S2A/F Tracker (1962–1979)	5	Maritime Patrol/ASW
Lockheed SP-2E/H Neptune (1977–1982)	6	Maritime Patrol/ASW
North American T-28F/P Fennec (1966–1978)	23	Advanced trainer/light attack
Lockheed L-188PF Electra (1973–1998)	3	Personnel & cargo transport, maritime surveillance
Douglas C-47 Skytrain (1946–1979)	2	Transport
Douglas C-54 Skymaster (1947–1976)	7	Transport
Grumman UH-16B Albatross (1960–1977)	4	SAR/ASW
Beechcraft C-45H (1961–1978)	15	Transport

Table 9: Argentine Naval Aviation aircraft types on strength in the mid-1970s[6] *(continued)*		
Beechcraft C-45J (1966–1980)	2	Transport
De Havilland Canada DHC-6-200 (1968–1977)	1	Transport/air photography
Hawker HS-125 Series 400B (1972–1994)	1	VIP Transport
Beechcraft Queen Air B-80 (1971–1992)	5	Light transport/air photography
Pilatus PC-6B/H2 Turbo Porter (1971–present)	3	Multipurpose/light transport
Aerospatiale SA.316B Alouette III (1969–2010)	10	Multipurpose/light attack
Sikorsky S-61D-4 Sea King (1971–present)	5	ASW/transport

Some of the aircraft types used by the Naval Aviation in the mid-1970s. Clockwise, Douglas A-4Q Skyhawk, Aermacchi MB.326GB Pelican, Grumman S2A Tracker and Lockheed SP2 Neptune. (Adolfo Soto, *Amilarg*, COAN, Dick Lohuis)

Marine Infantry Command (*Comando de la Infantería de Marina*)

The Marine Infantry Command was structured in companies of 150 men, with each section (platoon) having 36 troops. A battalion was made up of three Marine Infantry companies and other logistics, support and services troops, between 800 and 900 effectives.

Argentine Marines were armed with FN49, FAL and Garand M1 rifles. They were organised as shown in Table 10.

Table 10: Organisation of Marine Infantry Command (*Comando de la Infantería de Marina*)		
Unit	**Base**	**Province**
Marine Infantry Battalion No. 1 (BIM.1)	Río Gallegos	Santa Cruz
Marine Infantry Battalion No. 2 (BIM.2) *Capitán de Fragata D. Pedro Edgardo Giachino*	Baterías Marine Infantry Base, Punta Alta	Buenos Aires
Marine Infantry Battalion No. 3 (BIM.3) *Almirante Eleazar Videla*	Zárate Naval Base	Buenos Aires
Marine Infantry Battalion No. 4 (BIM.4)	Ushuaia Naval Base	Tierra del Fuego
Marine Infantry No. 5 (BIM.5)	Río Grande	Tierra del Fuego
Amphibious Commando Group	Puerto Belgrano Naval Base	Buenos Aires
Combat Support Service (SPAC)	Punta Alta	Buenos Aires
Security Battalion of the General Staff of the Navy	Libertad Building	Buenos Aires city
Security Battalion of the Puerto Belgrano Naval Base	Puerto Belgrano	Buenos Aires
Command and Logistics Support Battalion	Puerto Belgrano	Buenos Aires
Amphibious Vehicle Battalion No. 1	Baterías Marine Infantry Base in Punta Alta	Buenos Aires

Table 10: Organisation of Marine Infantry Command (*Comando de la Infantería de Marina*) (*continued*)		
Communications Battalion No. 1	Puerto Belgrano Naval Base	Buenos Aires
Field Artillery Battalion No. 1	Puerto Belgrano Naval Base	Buenos Aires
Anti-aircraft Battalion	Puerto Belgrano Naval Base	Buenos Aires
Amphibious Engineers Company	Puerto Belgrano Naval Base	Buenos Aires

In 1972, the Argentine Navy incorporated 21 AMTRAC LVTP-7A1 amphibious tracked vehicles (generically called VAO, *Vehículo anfibio a oruga*, Tracked Amphibious Vehicle), of which 19 were personnel carriers (LVTP-7), one command (LVTC-7), and one recovery (LVTR-7). Its main armament was a 12.7mm M85 machine gun located in a 360-degree rotating turret. During the 1970s, faced with the need to modernise its amphibious capacity, the Navy also incorporated 15 LARC-5 wheeled amphibious vehicles (VAR, *Vehículo Anfibio a Ruedas*, Wheeled Amphibious Vehicle). These served with Amphibious Vehicle Battalion No. 1

The Marines also had 12 Thomson Brandt MO120 AM50 heavy mortars, 30 81mm mortars and 45 60mm mortars. As anti-tank weapons they had Bantam missiles, 105mm and 75mm recoilless guns and Instalaza 88.9mm rocket launchers. They also had six M114 155mm howitzers and 12 M101 105mm howitzers.

Argentine Coast Guard (*Prefectura Naval Argentina*)

The Argentine Coast Guard (*Prefectura Naval Argentina*/PNA), a force under the Commander-in-Chief of the Navy, acted as a police service for security in navigation, as well as customs auxiliary police. It had jurisdiction over the seas, rivers, lagoons, lakes, and canals throughout the territory, including Antarctica and the islands of the South Atlantic.

The PNA was organised into a National Prefecture, National Sub-prefecture, directorates, departments, services, zone prefectures, prefectures, sub-prefectures and institutes. At that time, the command of the PNA was exercised by an Admiral of the Argentine Navy with the title of General Prefect.

The country was divided into 10 Naval Prefectures:

Upper Paraná River Zone (headquarters in Posadas)
Upper Uruguay River Zone (Pasos de los Libres)
Lower Paraná River Zone (Rosario)
Lower Uruguay River Zone (Concepción del Uruguay)
Delta Zone (Tigre)
Lacustre and Comahue Zone (Neuquén)
North Argentine Sea Zone (Bahía Blanca)
South Argentine Sea Zone (Río Gallegos)
Río de la Plata Zone (Buenos Aires)
Superior Paraná and Paraguay River Zone (Corrientes)

Argentine Marines during manoeuvres. (*La Gaceta Marinera*)

In the mid-1970s there were two Coast Guard boats (CG-13 PNA *Delfín* and GC-47 PNA *Tonina*), three speedboats (GC-21 PNA *Lynch*, GC-22 PNA *Toll* and GC-33 PNA *Erezcano*), a river boat (CG-34 PNA *Dorado*), a tug (CG-41 PNA *Rawson*), eight Type 48 speedboats (GC-48 to GC-55) and other small vessels. Its larger boats, the frigate GC-11 PNA *Azopardo* (ex-Argentine

The Coast Guard minesweeper PNA *Spiro* (GC-12). (*Histarmar* Archives)

A Coast Guard Aviation Shorts SC-7 Skyvan 3M-500. (Alberto Martín)

Navy ARA *Hércules*) and the minesweeper GC-12 PNA *Spiro* (ex-Argentine Navy ARA *Spiro*), were about to be retired from active service.

Coast Guard Aviation (*Aviación de la Prefectura Naval Argentina*)

In 1970, the Aviation of the Argentine Coast Guard became dependent on the Directorate of Zone Prefectures under the designation of the Aviation Division. It was reorganised as follows: Headquarters, Operations Section, Maintenance Section, Accounting Section, Secretariat, Office and Personnel Section and Communications Section. During the 1970s, the air fleet was also renewed with the acquisition of five Shorts SC-7 Skyvan 3M-400s, which replaced the De Havilland D.H. 104 Dove and Douglas DC-3 aircraft. They were in active service from 1971–1993. Six Hughes 369HS helicopters were also acquired, which replaced the Bell 47G/J. The Hughes helicopters were in active service from 1968–1988. In 1972, a central heliport was built in Dock F of the Port of Buenos Aires, with two hangars. The Skyvans belonged to the Fixed Wing Squadron and the Hughes to the Rotary Wing Squadron.

Argentine Army (*Ejército Argentino*)

In 1972, the Argentine Army created its Internal Framework Capacities Plan (*Plan de Capacidades Marco Interno*), which divided Argentine territory into four defence zones plus the area of the federal capital, for the fight against terrorism. These zones coincided with the natural jurisdictions of the Army Corps.

The Commanders-in-Chief of the Argentine Army in the 1970s were as shown in Table 11.[7]

Table 11: Commanders of the Army in the 1970s

Officer	Term
Lieutenant General Jorge Raúl Carcagno	25 May 1973 to 19 December 1973
Lieutenant General Leandro Enrique Anaya	19 December 1973 to 13 May 1975
Lieutenant General Alberto Numa Laplane	13 May 1975 to 27 August 1975
Lieutenant General Jorge Rafael Videla	27 August 1975 to 31 July 1978
Lieutenant General Roberto Eduardo Viola	31 July 1978 to 29 December 1979

The Argentine Army was divided into five corps (one of them deactivated) that covered the entire nation. Each corps or division was made up of brigades, and these, in turn, comprised regiments, detachments and auxiliary groups. As of October 1975, in accordance with the General Commander of the Army's Directive No. 404/75, the Argentine armed forces assumed operational control of the

The Argentine Army had five Commanders-in-Chief between 1973 and 1979. From left to right, Lieutenant Generals Jorge Raúl Carcagno, Leandro Enrique Anaya, Alberto Numa Laplane, Jorge Rafael Videla and Roberto Eduardo Viola. (Open Source)

President María Estela Martínez de Perón and the Director of the Nation Military School, Brigadier General José Antonio Vaquero, during the anniversary ceremony of that school on 11 October 1974. (Open Source)

Some of the senior generals of the Argentine Army: Major General Carlos Guillermo Suárez Mason (I Army Corps), Major General Ramón Genaro Díaz Bessone (II Army Corps), Major General Luciano Benjamín Menéndez (III Army Corps), Brigadier General Osvaldo René Azpitarte (V Army Corps) and Brigadier General Santiago Omar Riveros (Military Institutes Command). (Open Source)

entire country in the fight against terrorist subversion. The country was divided into five operational zones that were structured on the pre-existing jurisdictions of the respective Argentine Army corps. Each zone was divided into sub-zones, and these into areas and sub-areas. The Army had primary responsibility in each zone, with the support of the Air Force and the Navy, and the subordination of all federal or provincial security forces (police, Gendarmerie and penal institutions).

In the mid-1970s, the Argentine Army was organised as shown in Table 12.[8]

Table 12: Argentine Army Corps

Corps	Headquarters:	Commander:	Jurisdiction:	Military Unit	City
I Army Corps	Palermo Barracks, Buenos Aires	Major General Alberto Numa Laplane (1975), Major General Rodolfo Eugenio Cánepa (1975), Major General Carlos Guillermo Suárez Mason (1976–1978)	Defence Zone 1: Provinces of Buenos Aires and La Pampa	101st Armoured Cavalry Exploration Detachment	Toay
				101st Artillery Group	Junín
				101st Intelligence Detachment	La Plata
				102nd Intelligence Detachment	Tandil
				101st Air Defence Artillery Group	Ciudadela
				X Mechanised Infantry Brigade	La Plata
				I Armoured Cavalry Brigade	Tandil
II Army Corps *Teniente General Juan Carlos Sánchez*	Army Garrison in Rosario, province of Santa Fé	Major General Roberto Viola (1975), Major General Ramón Genaro Díaz Bessone (1976), Major General Leopoldo Fortunato Galtieri (1977–1978)	Defence Zone 2: Provinces of Formosa, Chaco, Misiones, Corrientes, Santa Fé and Entre Ríos	121st Command Communication Battalion	Mercedes
				III Infantry Brigade	Curuzú Cuatiá
				VII Mountain Infantry Brigade	Corrientes
				II Armoured Cavalry Brigade	Paraná
III Army Corps *Ejército del Norte*	Army Garrison in Córdoba	Major General Luciano Benjamín Menéndez (1975–1979)	Defence Zone 3: Provinces of Córdoba, San Luis, Mendoza, San Juan, La Rioja, Catamarca, Santiago del Estero, Tucumán, Salta and Jujuy	IV Airborne Infantry Brigade	Córdoba
				V Mountain Infantry Brigade	Salta
				VIII Mountain Infantry Brigade	Mendoza
				V Infantry Brigade	Tucumán
IV Army Corps (deactivated)					
V Army Corps *Teniente General Julio Argentino Roca*	Army Garrison in Bahía Blanca	Brigadier General Osvaldo René Azpitarte (1976–1977), Brigadier General José Antonio Vaquero (1977–1979)	Defence Zone 5: Provinces of Neuquén, Río Negro, the south of the province of Buenos Aires, Chubut, Santa Cruz and Tierra del Fuego	VI Infantry Brigade	Neuquén
				IX Mechanised Cavalry Brigade	Comodoro Rivadavia

Table 12: Argentine Army Corps *(continued)*

<table>
<tr><td rowspan="12">Argentine Army Command of Military Institutes</td><td rowspan="12">Army Garrison in Campo de Mayo</td><td rowspan="12">Brigadier General Santiago Omar Riveros (1975–1979)</td><td rowspan="12">Defence Zone 4: Federal capital (city of Buenos Aires)</td><td>School of Engineers</td><td>Escobar and Tigre</td></tr>
<tr><td>School of Communications</td><td>San Isidro</td></tr>
<tr><td>Cavalry School</td><td>General San Martín</td></tr>
<tr><td>Artillery School</td><td>San Fernando</td></tr>
<tr><td>Infantry School</td><td>Vicente López</td></tr>
<tr><td>Sargento Carbral NCO School</td><td>Pilar</td></tr>
<tr><td>General Lemos Combat Support Services School</td><td>General Sarmiento</td></tr>
<tr><td>Army Military School</td><td>Tres de Febrero</td></tr>
<tr><td>Military Intelligence School</td><td>Zárate</td></tr>
</table>

Each infantry brigade was made up of three regiments, an artillery group, squadrons and companies, totalling approximately 4,000 troops. In the mid-1970s, the Argentine Army had 10 infantry brigades, two airborne infantry brigades, two mountain brigades, two armoured cavalry (tanks) brigades, two mountain infantry brigades and a mixed infantry and armoured cavalry brigade.

The Argentine Army's regiments each comprised three companies of infantry, a commando company and a support services company, to which was added a group of heavy weapons or artillery, making a total of 700 troops. Each company was made up of 150 men, grouped as four infantry sections (platoons) and one heavy weapons section. Each infantry section consisted of between 30 and 35 soldiers. The brigade was the largest unit in the Argentine Army, consisting of approximately 2,200–2,500 men organised into two or three infantry regiments and one cavalry regiment, or three cavalry regiments (in the armoured brigades). To the regiments were added an artillery group (field or anti-aircraft), a logistics battalion and another for services.

Argentine Army personnel of Artillery Group GA101. (*Ejécito Argentino*)

Infantry soldiers pose with a commanding officer in front of a M3 half-track vehicle (left). Another group of soldiers with FAL assault rifles in the mid-1970s (right). (*Ejército Argentino*)

Close-combat exercises in 1976. The 'enemy' soldiers wore the old Swiss helmet and a different-coloured shirt. (*Ejército Argentino*)

Armoured vehicles of the Argentine Army. Clockwise, Sherman IVC Firefly tank, M4 Sherman with 76mm cannon, AMX-13 *Modéle 58* tank with 105mm gun and M113A1 armoured personnel carrier. The difficult terrain in the province of Tucumán prevented the use of armoured vehicles in combat there. (*Ejército Argentino*)

The light weapons carried by Argentine Army troops included 9mm Browning pistols, FN49s, Garand-Beretta BM59s, Belgian FN FAL rifles and locally manufactured PAM-2 and FM MAG 60-20 submachine guns. Two other models were locally manufactured, the FM MAG 60-30 to be mounted on helicopters and the FM MAG 60-40 for tanks. There were also Halcón ML-63 machine guns, Ithaca 37 shotguns, Bataan 54 and 71 shotguns and Browning M2 heavy machine guns. Troops could also be armed with Mk.1 hand grenades and Instalaza 65 rocket launchers. Three types of recoilless guns were available: the 105mm FM Czekalski model 1968–70, 75mm M20 and DGFM 75mm gun built in Argentina. There were also Cobra 2000, Bofors RB53 Bantam and the locally manufactured Mathogo 1 and 2 anti-tank missiles.

The howitzers available for the field artillery units were the 75mm Bofors L40 Argentine Model 1935, 105mm Oto Melara M56, 105mm M2A1, 155mm Schneider L15 and L30 Argentine Model 1928. Anti-aircraft artillery consisted of 40mm Bofors L60 Model 1936, 40mm Bofors L70/40, 30mm Hispano Suiza HS.831 and 20mm Oerlikon Type S model 1938 guns.

Table 13: Argentine Army armoured vehicles in service in the mid-1970s[9]		
Armoured vehicle	**Number of vehicles**	**Year of acquisition**
Sherman IVC/VC Firefly tank w/QF 17-pdr 76.2mm gun	206	1946
Sherman M4 tank w/76mm cannon OQF (Ordnance Quick Firing)	154	1948
Universal Carrier T-16	250	1948
M3, M5A1 and M9A1 half-track	320	Late 1940s
AMX-13 *Modéle 58* tank with 105mm gun	60	1967
AMX F3 155mm self-propelled gun	24	1967
AMX-13 VCPC armoured personnel carrier	41	1967
AMX-LP DPD bridge layer	2	1967
M113A1 armoured personnel carrier	250	1967–1969
M577A1 command-post carrier	10	1967–969
M548A1 tracked cargo carrier	12	1967–1969
AML-90 Panhard armoured scout vehicle with 90mm gun	60	1977–1978
Mowag Grenadier amphibious vehicle with 7.62mm MAG MG	30	1967–1968
Mowag Roland amphibious vehicle with 20mm Oerlikon AA gun	30	1967–1968
LARC-5 amphibious vehicle (VAR)	10	1972

Army units in the 1970s used a good number of modernised REO M35s trucks. The Army also had large numbers of Mercedes Benz Unimog 421 and model 2624 trucks, and M38A1 Jeeps and Ford M151 MUTTs were also used. In 1967, through what was known as the Europe Plan, AMX-VCPC infantry transport vehicles and AMX-LP (DPD) bridge layers were acquired.

The Argentine Army made extensive use of Mercedes Benz Unimog 421 trucks in the theatre of operations in Tucumán (top left). Another model widely used was the Mercedez Benz 2624 (top right). An old REO M35 truck pulling a 155mm Citer gun (bottom left) and a group of Ford M151 MUTT vehicles (bottom right). (*Ejército Argentino*)

Army Aviation (*Aviación del Ejército Argentino*)

The Argentine Army Aviation grew remarkably during the 1970s, as can be seen in Table 14.[10] Its headquarters was in the Libertad Building in Buenos Aires, but its main base was in Campo de Mayo Army Garrison and it was known as Army Aviation Battalion 601, with five companies: Commando, General Support, Assault Helicopter, Maintenance and Service. In October 1972, the Flight Instruction Division was created for the training of Army fixed-wing aircraft and helicopter pilots. Army pilots were also trained as technical specialists for maintenance tasks.

Table 14: Argentine Army Aviation aircraft types in service in the mid-1970s

Type	In service	Number of aircraft	Role
De Havilland DHC-6-200/300 Twin Otter	1968–present	4	Light transport
Beechcraft King Air 100	1970–1994	1	Light transport
Rockwell Sabreliner 75A	1974–2014	1	VIP transport
Piper PA-23-250 Aztec	1964–1980	4	Light transport
Beechcraft 65 Queen Air B-80	1967–present	4	Light transport
Beechcraft 100 King Air	1970–1994	1	Light transport
Cessna T207 Turbo Skywagon	1976–2018	9	Light transport
Cessna U.17A Skywagon	1957–1998	11	Liaison
Piper L-21B Super Cub	1957–1977	8	Primary trainer/liaison
Cessna T-41D Mescalero	1974–present	5	Primary trainer/liaison
Bell OH-13H/S Sioux	1965–1978	6	Utility helicopter/trainer
Bell UH-1H Huey	1970–present	26	Troop transport
Bell 212	1976–present	2	Troop transport
Aerospatiale AS315B Lama	1975–present	6	Utility helicopter/SAR
Fairchild-Hiller FH-1100	1968–1980	7	Trainer/observation

Argentine National Gendarmerie (*Gendarmeria Nacional Argentina*)

Together with the Federal Police, the Naval Coast Guard and the Airport Security Police, the National Gendarmerie constituted the Federal Security Forces of Argentina. Through Law 18,711 of 17 June 1970, the Board of Commanders-in-Chief of the Argentine Revolution imposed on the National Gendarmerie police powers that had been the responsibility of the Commander-in-Chief of the Army. On 25 November 1971, the regime promulgated a new law for the Gendarmerie, with it passing from the command of the Commander-in-Chief of the Army to the Gendarmerie Commander, an Army officer with a rank not lower than brigadier general.

The National Gendarmerie participated in Operation Independence in 1975, led by the Argentine Army, by order of

Aircraft of the Argentine Army widely used in Operation Independence. Clockwise, Bell UH-1H, Piper L-21B, Cessna T207 and De Havilland Canada DHC-6 Twin Otter. (*Ejército Argentino*)

Army Aviation flight platform in Campo de Mayo in 1974. Note the aircraft in service at the time: DHC-6 Twin Otter, Cessna U.17A, Piper L-21B and Bell UH-1H, FH-1100 and OH-13H helicopters (above). Army Aviation Bell OH-13H helicopters were used for basic training between 1965 and 1978 (below). (*Ejército Argentino*)

President María Estela Martínez de Perón. On 28 August of that year, the Air Force C-130E Hercules serial TC-62, carrying 114 gendarmes, was brought down by a bomb installed on the runway of *Teniente Benjamín Matienzo* Airport. A total of six gendarmes lost their lives in this incident.

During the regime of the National Reorganisation Process, which began with the *coup d'état* of 24 March 1976, the National Gendarmerie participated in acts of repression, in collaboration with the Argentine armed forces.

The Gendarmerie had checkpoints all over the country, with its own fleet of transport and support vehicles, including horses for areas with difficult vehicle access, dogs trained for security and rescue, and a fleet of fixed-wing aircraft and helicopters.

The Gendarmerie was divided into several sections: Operations, Security and Defence, Aviation, Intelligence, Criminalistics and Forensic Studies, Personnel, Health, Education, Logistics, Maintenance and Training. The Gendarmerie forces were deployed in five regions: Region I (Headquarters: Campo de Mayo, province of Buenos Aires), Region II (Rosario, province of Santa Fé), Region III (Córdoba, province of Córdoba), Region IV (Salta, province of Salta) and Region V (Bahía Blanca, province of Buenos Aires). The Air Transport Division of the National Gendarmerie, which had its main base in Campo de Mayo, had aircraft on strength in the mid-1970s as shown in Table 15.[11]

Members of the Argentine National Gendarmerie in combat gear, about to board an Air Force C-130 bound for Tucumán in 1976. (*Gendarmería Nacional Argentina*)

Argentine National Gendarmerie troops. (*Gendarmería Nacional Argentina*)

Table 15: Argentine National Gendarmerie aircraft types in service in the mid-1970s			
Type	**In service**	**Number of aircraft**	**Role**
Cessna 182H Skylane	1965–present	6	Border patrol/liaison/trainer
Cessna 185A Skywagon	1962–1986	1	Trainer
Cessna U206 Super Skywagon	1974–present	3	Border patrol/liaison
Cessna 210 Centurion	1962–1979	1	Border patrol/liaison
Cessna 310G/H	1962–1986	2	Border patrol/liaison
Cessna 337 Super Skymaster	1965–1986	2	Border patrol/liaison
Cessna 402 Utililiner	1976–1994	1	VIP transport
Piper PA-18 Super Cub	1968–present	3	Trainer/light transport
Piper PA-23-250 Aztec	1973–present	4	Trainer/light transport
Piper PA-31-310B Navajo	1975–present	3	Border patrol/transport
Piper PA-31T Cheyenne II	1975–present	1	Border patrol/transport
Fairchild-Hiller FH-1100	1976–1985	2	Trainer/SAR
Bell 47G-3B-1 Sioux	1967–1984	2	Trainer/SAR
N.B. Gendarmerie aircraft have the registration GN- plus the serial number			

Two types of aircraft used by the National Gendarmerie, the Fairchild-Hiller FH-1100 and Cessna U206. (Horacio Gareiso via Vladimiro Cettolo, Michael Magnusson)

Argentine Federal Police (*Policía Federal Argentina*)

The Argentine Federal Police (PFA/ *Policía Federal Argentina*) was created on 24 December 1943 and began operating on 1 January 1945. Each of the 23 provinces into which Argentina is divided also has its own police force, as established by the national constitution, with the title of Provincial Police. In the 1970s, the heads of the PFA were as shown in Table 16.[12]

Table 16: Heads of the Argentine Federal Police in the 1970s

Chief of the Argentine Federal Police (PFA)	Term
Army Brigadier General (Ret.) Miguel Ángel Iñíguez	24 September 1973 to 10 May 1974
General Commissioner Alberto Villar (*)	11 May 1974 to 01 November 1974
General Commissioner Luis Margaride	08 November 1974 to 18 August 1975
General Commissioner Omar Enrique Pinto	18 August 1975 to 06 February 1976
Army Major General Albano Harguindeguy	06 February 1976 to 24 March 1976
Army Brigadier General Cesáreo Ángel Cardozo (+)	04 April 1976 to 18 June 1976
Army Brigadier General Arturo Amador Corbetta	23 June 1976 to 06 July 1976
Army Brigadier General René Edmundo Ojeda	13 July 1976 to 09 March 1979
(*) killed by guerrillas on 01.11.74 (see main text)	
(+) killed by a *Montoneros* bomb blast on 18.06.76 (see main text)	

According to the Organic Law of the Argentine Federal Police through Decree-Law Nr. 333 of 14 January 1958, the PFA had a Headquarters, Sub-headquarters and Superintendence. This structure included the following departments: Metropolitan Security, Criminal Investigation, Personnel, Technical, Federal Security, Directorate of Economic Criminal Investigation, Chief of Staff, Public Relations and Legal Issues.

At the end of 1970, the Aviation Department of the Argentine Federal Police was created, which came under the Metropolitan Security Superintendence. The first fixed-wing aircraft acquired was an FMA IA.50 Guaraní II in July 1971, with a second example in March 1972. Four MBB Bo 105A helicopters were incorporated in 1972, forming a Helicopter Squadron for aerial surveillance tasks, medevac and police procedures. An Aircraft Squadron was also

Some of the Chiefs of the Argentine Federal Police in the 1970s. From left to right, Brigadier General (Ret.) Miguel Ángel Iñíguez, General Commissioner Alberto Villar, General Commissioner Luis Margaride, Major General Albano Harguindeguy, Brigadier General Cesáreo Ángel Cardozo and Brigadier General Arturo Amador Corbetta. (PFA)

Two smiling young officers of the Argentine Federal Police in the 1970s (left). Police officers armed with shotguns aboard a Ford Falcon patrol car (right). (PFA)

An Argentine Federal Police MBB Bo 105A (left) and the FMA IA.50 Guaraní II registration LQ-JXN. (Caros Abella, Marcelo Miranda)

created for transport tasks. In 1977, a Cessna 206 Super Skywagon was purchased. It is worth mentioning that the first pilot police officers and mechanic NCOs were trained in the Army Aviation facilities at Campo de Mayo, but they were also trained at the National Institute of Civil Aviation (INAC), and later at the Aviation School of the Argentine Air Force in Córdoba and the Naval Aviation School in Punta Indio.

4

THE ERP AND *MONTONEROS* ORGANISATIONS

Although there were several subversive groups, as seen in Chapter 1 of this volume, there were two main guerrilla organisations that fought against the Argentine armed forces.

People's Revolutionary Army (*Ejército Revolucionario del Pueblo*/ERP)[1]

The People's Revolutionary Army (ERP) was the armed wing of the Workers' Revolutionary Party (PRT). The highest authority of the PRT was its National Congress, which functioned with three committees: the central, executive and provincial. Each provincial committee had regional committees, further divided into zones, fronts and cells.

The ERP had a Political-Military Committee, a General Staff – which was in charge of operations, international relations and communications – and a team from the command in charge of logistics, supply, health and propaganda.

In theory, the ERP military structure comprised battalions, but in reality they could only form urban and forest companies. Each company had a military chief with the rank of captain, a political chief (also a captain), a committee, a staff, a command platoon, a logistics platoon, a support platoon, and two assault platoons, in all comprising approximately 130 men. Each platoon was made up of between two and four squads, each led by a lieutenant, with a total of 37 troops. In turn, each squad had between eight and 12 combatants, led by a sergeant. It is estimated that the ERP had some 7,200 militants, along with about 20,000 sympathisers.

The General Commander of the ERP was Mario Roberto Santucho (known as *Roby*), the Operations Chief was Juan Manuel Carrizo (*Capitán Francisco*), the Intelligence Chief Juan Mangini (*Capitán Pepe*) and the Logistics Chief J.E. Ledesma (*Capitán Pedro*). By 1974, the ERP included the following companies:

The leadership of the ERP frequently offered press conferences, sometimes with their faces uncovered, as here with Gorriarán Merlo and Santucho (left), and other times wearing hoods. (Open Source)

- *Héroes de Trelew*, an urban company with operational jurisdiction in the federal capital and the province of Buenos Aires. Commander: Guillermo Raúl Pérez (known as *Benja* or *Benjamin*).
- *Decididos de Córdoba*, an urban company whose area was the province of Córboba and the north of the country. Commander: Eduardo Guillermo Castelo (known as *Hugo*).
- *Combate de San Lorenzo*, an urban company in the province of Santa Fé. Commander: Mario Emilio Delfino (known as *Cacho*).
- *Ramón Rosa Jiménez*, the only forest company, whose operations were in the province of Tucumán. Commander: Juan Manuel Carrizo (known as *Juanma*, *El Manco*, *El Legendario*, *El Flaco* or *Capitán Francisco*).
- *Héroes de 1917*, an urban company in Greater Buenos Aires. Commander: Enrique Luis Enrique Pujals (known as *Anibal* or *El Flaco Garay*).
- *España*, an urban company whose commander was Juan Arnold Kremer Balugano (known as *Luis Mattini*).
- *Nicaragua*, an urban company whose commander was Enrique Haroldo Gorriarán Merlo (known as *Comandante Ramón*, *Ricardo* or *El Pelado*).

Later, there were other urban companies – *Juan de Oliviera*, *José Luís Castrogiovanni* and *Guillermo Pérez*. One peculiarity of the organisation was that all the ERP's military formations were named after deceased combatants or for geographical locations.

The combatants carried FAL or Mauser rifles, Batan shotguns and hand grenades. Rifle squads had a leader with the rank of sergeant, who led between eight and 12 troops. A support platoon was led by a lieutenant and had a squad of machine-gunners, one with explosives and another with mortars and bazookas. They also had Madsen or MAG machine guns, one or two 60mm or 81mm mortars, some Energa grenade launchers, a bazooka, Vietnamese-type mines, trotyl and gelamon explosives with fuses and detonators, PAM submachine guns and pistols or revolvers.

The ERP also manufactured its own weapons. It had three factories, two of them for the production of portable weapons and the other for explosives. One arms factory was located in the province of Buenos Aires, in the town of San Justo, where security forces found 1,200 JCR1 model machine guns and evidence of the group having distributed 1,600 more such weapons. The other factory was in the town of Almirante Brown on Route 4. The explosives factory was located in Pilar, where 300 kilos of plastic explosive were found.

Members of the ERP were experts in setting booby traps. Their combatants wore olive green uniforms, very similar to those used by the Argentine Army, sometimes with identifying armbands. They also used military ranks: commander (one red star as rank insignia), captain (one yellow star), lieutenant (two black stars), sergeant (one black star) and combatant (no rank insignia).

In the case of the *Ramón Rosa Jiménez* Mountain Company, it had a General Staff, three combat platoons – *Dago* (with the *Guanziroli* and *Teniente Chiquito* Squads), *Irrutia* (with the *Sargento Mariano* and *Raúl Penayo* Squads) and *Teniente Reynoso* (with

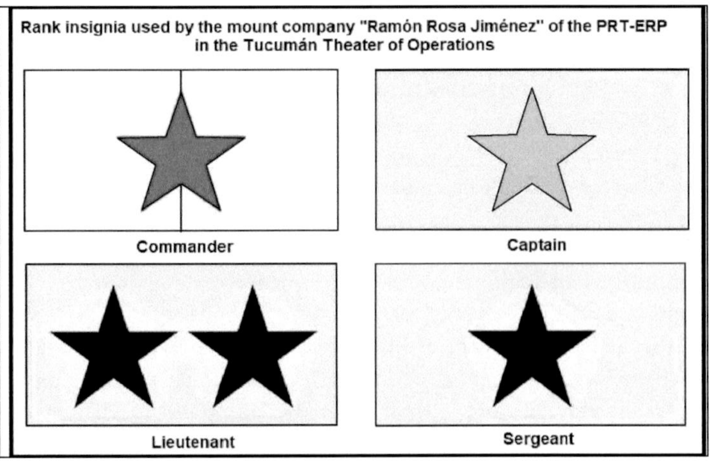

An ERP guerrilla camp in the Tucumán forests in 1975 (left). The 'military' ranks of the ERP (Commander: red on white; Captain gold on blue; Lieutenant and Sergeant black on blue) (right). (Open Source)

Two ERP technicians preparing hand grenades (left). An ERP platoon with its commander in the middle of the Tucumán jungle (right). (Open Source)

Just a few examples of the thousands of young Argentines deluded by an impossible dream carried out by a failed ideology. The ERP sold them the idea of a 'better homeland' and their young lives were cut short for nothing. Their *noms de guerre* included *Patricia*, *Rita*, *Beto*, *Palito*, *Simón*, *Petete*, *Gachi*, *Barba*, *Colorada*, *Horacio*, *Camilo*, *Juan Pablo*, *La Petisa*, *Negrita*, *Pata*, *Paraguayo*, *Lucho*, *Inés*, *Private Soldier*, *Tomás*, *Chiquito*, *La Espeche*, *El Francés*, *Lito* and *Tata*. (PFA)

On 15 December 1974, Carlos Héctor Germán, known as *Mauro Gómez*, a member of the ERP General Staff (centre, with a flag), presided over a formation in the middle of the Tucumán jungle. The escort with the rifle is *Sargento Dago*, a Chilean guerrilla from the MIR, who would die in the combat in Manchalá, and the one carrying the flagpole is Tomás Francisco Toconás, captured alive and later thrown from an Army helicopter in Santiago del Estero. (Open Source)

the *Vietnam Heroico* and *Explosivist* Squads) – and one platoon of logistics support.

Most combatants of the ERP were Argentine but a significant number came from abroad, especially from Cuba, Central America, Bolivia, Peru, from the disbanded *Tupamaros* gang of Uruguay and even from Eastern European countries.

They set up hideouts in the thick of the jungle with spare clothes, cleaning and medical supplies and canned food, which were guarded by sentries in nearby trees. Tactical communications were carried out through the use of modern American Handie-Talkie radios. Although most of its members had been fully indoctrinated by their leaders, there were significant numbers of defections, which in most cases carried a death sentence for 'betraying the cause'.

The national leadership of the *Montoneros* Party. From left to right, Commanders Mendizábal, Perdía, Firmenich and Yager, and Second Commanders Vaca Narvaja and Campiglia. (PFA)

One of the many *Montoneros* press conferences, with their leader, Firmenich (centre in light suit), before going into hiding. Note the photographs of Perón, Belgrano and Evita behind. (Open Source)

Ejército Montonero (Montonero Army)[2]

The *Montonero* Army was a subversive military organisation that was formed as the military arm of the *Montonero* Party. Its creation was the consequence of a reorganisation of the *Montoneros* political-military group carried out in 1975, which separated the political and military functions into two different organisations, although subordinating the military branch to political leadership. The *Montonero* Army was commanded from its creation until its dissolution by Mario Firmenich, known as *Pepe*. Its members wore uniforms and had ranks according to their hierarchy in the military chain of command. The creation of the *Montonero* Army was announced in March 1976, a few days before the *de facto* government known as the National Reorganisation Process was installed in Argentina. It is estimated that the total number of *Montoneros* subversives was around 2,500 troops and some 12,000 sympathisers. The *Montoneros* military organisation, under a centralised leadership, had regional units in various provinces in order to control the operation of all their effectives. Each region had a combat column, which in turn was divided into various basic combat units (UBC) or platoons, including a logistics unit. Specifically, the Tucumán Regional Unit had the so-called Column 21 with three UBCs – west, east and south – and a logistics UBC. It is estimated that around 30 combatants and between 150 and 200 *Montoneros* militants operated in the province of Tucumán, not counting sympathisers, in logistical and propaganda tasks.

The *Montoneros* had FAL light automatic rifles, the locally produced PAM submachine guns, FAP heavy machine guns, Madsen 7.65mm machine guns, Colt revolvers and, among others, the Bersa, Tala, Ballester Beretta, Astra and Parabellum Walther pistols. In their attacks, they also made extensive use of homemade explosives and Molotov cocktails. The *Montoneros* also manufactured weapons and explosives, they had five factories, three of which were for the production of portable weapons and one for explosives. One of the arms factories was in in the Villa Ballester district, with the others in the towns of Garín and Florida. The explosives plants were located in the towns of Carapachay and Villa Dominico.

Weapons clandestinely manufactured by the *Montoneros* included the following:

- JCR1 (*Junta de Coordinación Revolucionaria*, Revolutionary Coordination Board) submachine gun: 3,700 were produced.
- *Yarará* (the *Guaraní* language name of a poisonous snake) submachine gun: only 15 were manufactured.
- *Monto* (from the word *Montoneros*) submachine gun. This was a copy of the Swedish Carl Gustav submachine gun. Its parts were manufactured in several cities – Mar del Plata, Florida, Don Torcuato, Garín, Villa Ballester and the federal capital.
- Traction fuse SFM / ET-1: 700 were produced.

- SFM/G5 hand grenade: It is estimated that 4,200 were manufactured in facilities detected in Carapachay.
- G70A type grenade: 5,000 were produced. These were shaped charges suitable for piercing certain armour and masonry.
- SFM-G40 Strim type grenade: 250 were manufactured. These were similar to the G70A, but anti-personnel versions.
- SFM4 Tromblon grenade launcher: estimated quantity 250.
- SFM-LG22-MP grenade launcher. Approximately 1,000 were manufactured in the *José Sabino Navarro* military factory, which was captured and dismantled by the security forces on 16 October 1976.
- C-2 plastic explosive: produced in factories detected in Rosario, Lanús and Villa Dominico. They set up another factory in Brazil that was neutralised shortly after it was established, and the last one, in the city of Sidon, Lebanon, which they exchanged with the *Al Fatah* Palestine Liberation Organization for training courses in that country. The clandestine plants in Argentina had a production capacity of 80–90kg per month. Between 1976 and 1978, the central logistics unit, the name of the explosives production plant, produced 780kg of C2 and more than 1,500kg of medium strength explosives.

None of these factories and arms production plants were operational for more than two years, being quickly dismantled.

For military operations, the *Montonero* Army and its militias adopted a uniform of a light blue shirt, navy blue pants and a black beret. The rank insignia were the same as those of the Argentine Army. If operations were in forested areas, a camouflaged uniform was adopted.

The structure of the *Montonero* Army had two specific departments:

- A Logistics Department, which dealt with the design, production, distribution and storage of weapons and explosives, as well as their purchase. The department also covered health matters (surgical material, medical supplies, drugs and houses to operate on the wounded).
- The Information Service (SI), or Information Department, which detected enemy targets and created intelligence on them. They worked on specific sectors: foreign companies and the oligarchy, the Argentine armed forces, the police and also security forces collaborators. The results of their tasks were transmitted to the combat groups. The SI also had an organised network of clandestine informants – which was secret even from the rest of the militants, systematically and regularly providing information

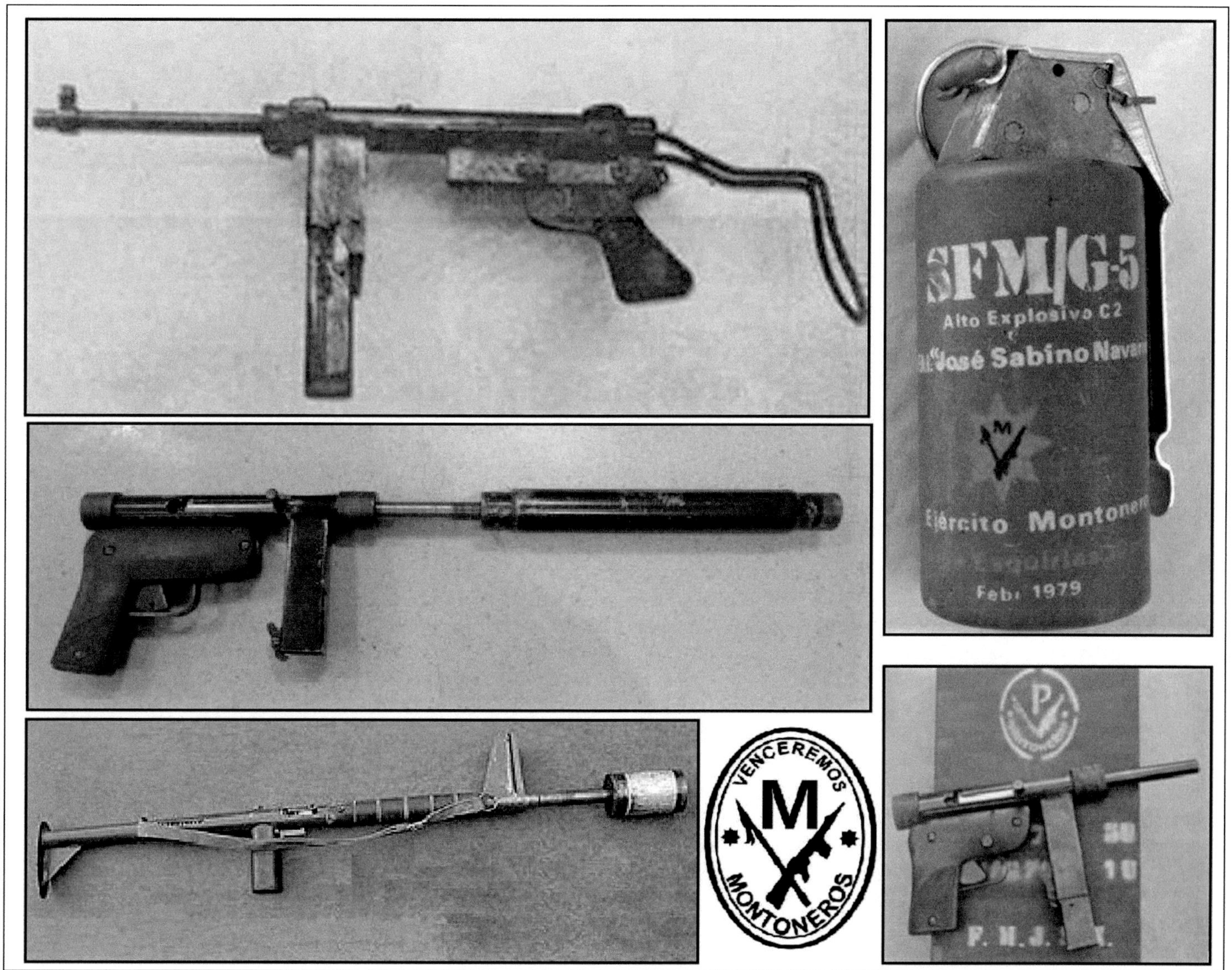

Some of the clandestinely manufactured weapons used by the ERP and *Montoneros*. The JCR1 submachine gun (top left), 9mm *Yarará* submachine gun with silencer (centre left), SFM-LG22-MP grenade launcher (bottom left), SFM/G5 hand grenade (top right) and *Monto* submachine gun (bottom right). (PFA)

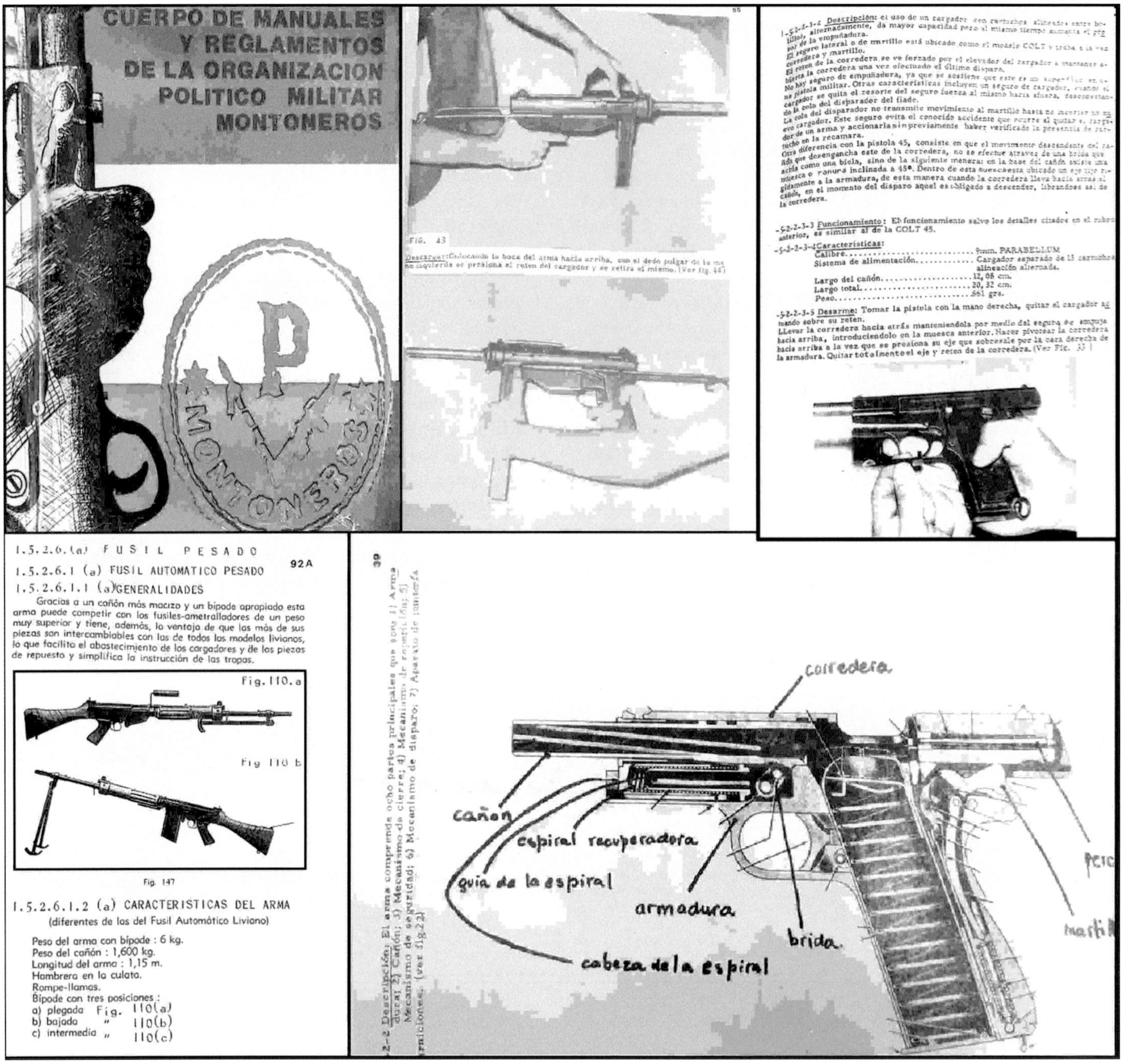

The *Montoneros* even published several manuals for the use of light and heavy arms and the manufacture of explosives to train the new troops incorporated into the subversive organisation. (PFA)

on enemy individuals and forces. They had infiltrators in all areas in which they operated, including thee armed forces, police, government, universities and factories.

Towards the end of 1976, the *Montoneros* had already launched its war against the armed forces, but its own army was still in the process of being constituted. The instruction plan for those who were to join in the fighting lasted for three or four days. It was carried out in a clandestine house, with a rifle, machine gun, 9mm pistols or .38 revolvers, grenades and grenade launchers. The instruction of the new recruits was the responsibility of each platoon leader. In addition, the new recruits had a series of manuals for the handling and use of different types of light and heavy weapons, the manufacture and use of bombs, guerrilla tactics, for example.

The military structure of the *Montoneros* was made up of combat sections, whose members were aspirants, led by a chief, who carried out combat actions. There were also militia companies, which were small units of four aspirants and a chief, who were in charge of harassment, propaganda, and sabotage actions. The military ranks of the *Montoneros* differed from those used by the ERP. They had a commander, and then senior officers, major officers, first and second officers, officers, aspirant officers, soldiers and militiamen. The *Montoneros* organisation was distributed throughout Argentina and had eight regional headquarters: Buenos Aires, Rosario, Santa Fé, Paraná, Cuyo, Córdoba, La Plata and Mar del Plata. Each regional headquarters was led by a senior officer and had several columns, each one under the command of a major officer.

The *Montoneros* carried out three tactical military offensives between 1974 and 1976:

- The first consisted of carrying out armed propaganda, as well as assassinating traitors to the Peronist cause and members of the security forces.

- In the second offensive, roadblocks, temporary control of urban areas and attacks on police stations were carried out. Attacks on the armed forces were also included.
- The last campaign was of withdrawal and preparation of a counter-offensive in the face of the annihilation campaign undertaken by the state security forces. During this period, the *Montoneros* carried out some 500 operations against the state.

After 1976, the group went into a progressive decline. Having mobilised large Peronist masses and shaken the country with their attacks, their leadership gradually lost its sense of reality, entering a spiral of indiscriminate violence that sentenced many of its militants to prison or death.

EPILOGUE

After the overthrow of General Perón in 1955, subversive groups had begun to appear and attacked the government of the Liberating Revolution. Those organisations were not limited to attacking the *de facto* governments but also the *de jure* ones, with the sole purpose of achieving the return of their leader Perón to Argentina. Such groups were widely encouraged and supported by former president Perón from exile, thus creating a monster that would be difficult for him to handle when he returned to Argentina in 1974 and assumed his third presidency. It was a long and painful process that caused hundreds of innocent victims, in addition to the casualties of the security forces and subversives themselves.

After the death of General Perón in July 1974 while serving as president, the situation in the country deteriorated to unprecedented levels in terms of violence, uncontrollable inflation, shortage of basic supplies, union disorganisation and extreme politicisation of schools and universities, which created a breeding ground that resulted in Operation Independence in February 1975 and finally the *coup d'état* of 24 March 1976 through which a military junta took over the government.

The actions of *Operativo Independencia*, the 1976 coup and the military – though not political – defeat of the guerrillas are covered in Volume 2 of this work.

APPENDICES

Table 17: Argentine Armed Forces ranks (officers)[1]		
Argentine Army	**Argentine Navy**	**Argentine Air Force**
Teniente General (Lieutenant General)	*Almirante* (Admiral)	*Brigadier General* (Brigadier General)
General de División (Major General)	*Vicealmirante* (Vice-Admiral)	*Brigadier Mayor* (Brigadier Major)
General de Brigada (Brigadier General)	*Contraalmirante* (Rear Admiral)	*Brigadier* (Brigadier)
Coronel Mayor (Colonel Major)	*Comodoro de Marina* (Commodore of the Navy)	*Comodoro Mayor* (Commodore Major)
Coronel (Colonel)	*Capitán de Navío* (Captain)	*Comodoro* (Commodore)
Teniente Coronel (Lieutenant Colonel)	*Capitán de Fragata* (Frigate Captain)	*Vicecomodoro* (Vice-Commodore)
Mayor (Major)	*Capitán de Corbeta* (Corvette Captain)	*Mayor* (Major)
Capitán (Captain)	*Teniente de Navío* (Ship Lieutenant)	*Capitán* (Captain)
Teniente Primero (1st Lieutenant)	*Teniente de Fragata* (Frigate Lieutenant)	*Primer Teniente* (1st Lieutenant)
Teniente (Lieutenant)	*Teniente de Corbeta* (Corvette Lieutenant)	*Teniente* (Lieutenant)
Subteniente (Sub-Lieutenant)	*Guardiamarina* (Midshipman)	*Alférez* (Ensign)

Table 18: Argentine Armed Forces ranks (NCOs)[2]		
Argentine Army	**Argentine Navy**	**Argentine Air Force**
Sub Oficial Mayor (Chief Warrant Officer)	*Sub Oficial Mayor* (Master Chief Petty Officer)	*Sub Oficial Mayor* (Chief Warrant Officer)
Sub Oficial Principal (Deputy Chief Officer)	*Sub Oficial Principal* (Deputy Chief Officer)	*Sub Oficial Principal* (Deputy Chief Officer)
Sargento Ayudante (Assistant Sergeant)	*Sub Oficial Primero* (Chief Warrant Officer)	*Sub Oficial Ayudante* (Assistant Chief Officer)
Sargento Primero (First Sergeant)	*Sub Oficial Segundo* (2nd Chief Warrant Officer)	*Sub Oficial Auxiliar* (Auxiliary Chief Officer)
Sargento (Sergeant)	*Cabo Principal* (Chief Corporal)	*Cabo Principal* (Chief Corporal)
Cabo Primero (First Corporal)	*Cabo Primero* (First Corporal)	*Cabo Primero* (First Corporal)
Cabo (Corporal)	*Cabo Segundo* (Second Corporal)	*Cabo Segundo* (Second Corporal)

Table 19: Argentine Armed Forces ranks (troops)[3]		
Argentine Army	**Argentine Navy**	**Argentine Air Force**
Cadete (Cadet)	*Cadete* (Cadet)	*Cadete* (Cadet)
Aspirante (Aspirant)	*Aspirante* (Aspirant)	*Aspirante* (Aspirant)
Dragoneante (Dragoneant)	*Dragoneante* (Dragoneant)	*Dragoneante* (Dragoneant)
Soldado (Soldier)	*Conscripto* (Conscript)	*Soldado* (Soldier)

Table 20: Argentine Coast Guard ranks[4]	
Officers	**NCOs**
Prefecto General (General Prefect)	*Ayudante Mayor* (Senior Assistant)
Prefecto Mayor (Senior Prefect)	*Ayudante Principal* (Chief Assistant)
Prefecto Principal (Chief Prefect)	*Ayudante de Primera* (First Assistant)
Prefecto (Prefect)	*Ayudante de Segunda* (Second Assistant)
Sub Prefecto (Deputy Prefect)	*Ayudante de Tercera* (Third Assistant)
Oficial Principal (Chief Officer)	*Cabo Primero* (First Corporal)
Oficial Auxiliar (Auxiliary Officer)	*Cabo Segundo* (Second Corporal)
Oficial Ayudante (Assistant Officer)	*Marinero* (Sailor)

Table 21: Argentine National Gendarmerie ranks[5]	
Officers	**NCOs**
Comandante General (General Commander)	*Sub Oficial Mayor* (Chief Warrant Officer)
Comandante Mayor (Senior Commander)	*Sub Oficial Principal* (Deputy Chief Officer)
Comandante Principal (Main Commander)	*Sargento Ayudante* (Assistance Sergeant)
Segundo Comandante (Second Commander)	*Sargento Primero* (First Sergeant)
Primer Alférez (First Ensign)	*Sargento* (Sergeant)
Alférez (Ensign)	*Cabo Primero* (First Corporal)
Subalférez (Deputy Ensign)	*Cabo* (Corporal)
Cadete (Cadet)	*Aspirante a Sub Oficial* (NCO Aspirant)
-	*Gendarme* (Gendarme)
-	*Gendarme de Segunda* (Second-Class Gendarme)

Table 22: Argentine Federal Police ranks[6]	
Officers	**NCOs**
Comisario General (General Commissioner)	*Sub Oficial Mayor* (Chief Warrant Officer)
Comisario Mayor (Senior Commissioner)	*Sub Oficial Auxiliar* (Assistant Warrant Officer)
Comisario Inspector (Inspector Commissioner)	*Sub Oficial Escribiente* (NCO)
Comisario (Commissioner)	*Sargento Primero* (First Sergeant)
Sub Comisario (Deputy Commissioner)	*Sargento* (Sergeant)
Principal (Principal)	*Cabo Primero* (First Corporal)
Inspector (Inspector)	*Cabo* (Corporal)
Sub Inspector (Deputy Inspector)	*Agente* (Agent)
Ayudante (Assistant)	*Aspirante* (NCO Aspirant)
-	*Cadete* (Cadet)

Table 23: Guerrilla organisation ranks[7]		
ERP		***Montoneros***
Officers, NCOs & effectives	Rank Insignia	Officers & Troops
Comandante (Commander)	One red star	*Comandante* (Commander)
Capitán (Captain)	One yellow star	*Oficial Superior* (Senior Officer)
Teniente (Lieutenant)	Two black stars	*Oficial Mayor* (Major Officer)
Sargento (Sergeant)	One black star	*Oficial Primero* (First Officer)
Combatiente (Combatant)	No rank insignia	*Oficial Segundo* (Second Officer)
-	-	*Oficial* (Officer)
-	-	*Aspirante a Oficial* (Aspirant Officer)
-	-	*Soldado* (Soldier)
-	-	*Miliciano* (Militiaman)

BIBLIOGRAPHY

Books

Amores Oliver, Eduardo Juan, *Guía de Aeronaves Militares 1912–2006. Fuerza Aérea Argentina* (Buenos Aires: Dirección de Estudios Históricos de la. Fuerza Aérea Argentina, 2007)

Aranda Durañona, Comodoro (Ret.) Oscar Luis, *El Vuelo del Cóndor. Fuerza Aérea Argentina. 1912–2012. Cien años protegiendo nuestro cielo* (Buenos Aires: Dirección de Estudios Históricos de la Fuerza Aérea Argentina, 2012)

Baldini, Atilio, & Bontti, Sergio, *El SA.315B Lama en la Fuerza Aérea Argentina, 1ª Edición* (Mendoza: Inca Editorial Cooperativa de Trabajo Ltda, 2003)

Baldini, Atilio & Núñez Padín, Jorge F., *North American F-86F-30-NA Sabre, Serie Fuerza Aérea #16* (Bahía Blanca: Ediciones Jorge Félix Núñez Padín, 2009)

Burzaco, Ricardo, *Infierno en el Monte Tucumano. Argentina 1973–1976* (Buenos Aires: Buró Editor S.A., 2nd Edition, 1997)

Caballero, Dr Ricardo, & Cater, Phil, *The Pucará Story*, MMP Books, White Series No. 9121 (Sandomierz, Poland: Stratus s.c., 2013)

Carballo, Comisario (Ret.) Walter Hugo, *Alas Azules. Historia de la Aeronáutica Policial* (Buenos Aires: AMT Ediciones, 2016)

Carreras, Julio: *La política armada: Una historia de las guerrillas del Siglo XX en la Argentina* (Kindle Edition, 2014)

Caviasca, Guillermo, *Guerra Contrarrevolucionaria en Tucumán. La guerrilla frente al Ejército según 'El diario del General Acdel Edgardo Vilas'* (Buenos Aires: Editorial Cooperativa El Río Suena, 2021)

Cicalesi, Juan Carlos, & Rivas, Santiago, *FMA IA.58 Pucará*, Serie Fuerza Aérea #18 (Bahía Blanca: Ediciones Jorge Félix Núñez Padín, 2010)

De Santis, Daniel Héctor, *A vencer o morir. Historia del PRT-ERP. Documentos*, Volumes 1 & 2 (Buenos Aires: Nuestra América, Volume 1, 2004, Volume 2, 2006)

Díaz Bessone, General de División Ramón Genaro, *Guerra Revolucionaria en la Argentina* (Buenos Aires: Editorial Círculo Militar, 1988)

Fernández Zicavo, Jorge, *Guerra Revolucionaria Argentina (1969–1979)* (Kindle Edition, 2016)

Galasso, Norberto, *Perón. Serie Grandes Biografías. Volume 1: Formación, ascenso y caída (1893–1955), Volume 2: Exilio, resistencia, retorno y muerte (1955–1974).* (Buenos Aires: Editorial Colihue, 2005)

Gillespie, Richard, *Soldados de Perón. Historia Crítica sobre los Montoneros* (Buenos Aires: Editorial Sudamericana, 2008)

González Breard, Coronel Eusebio, *La Guerrilla en Tucumán. Una historia no escrita* (Buenos Aires: Editorial Círculo Militar, 2001)

Gutman, Daniel, *Sangre en el monte. La increíble aventura del ERP en los cerros tucumanos* (Buenos Aires: Editorial Sudamericana, 2011)

Lewis, Paul H, *The 'Dirty War' in Argentina* (Westport, Connecticut: Praeger Publishers, 2002)

Luna, Félix, *De Perón a Lanusse 1943–1973* (Buenos Aires: Editorial Planeta, 4th Edition, 1987)

Manfroni, Carlos A., & Villarruel, Victoria E., *Los otros muertos. Las víctimas civiles del terrorismo guerrillero de los 70* (Buenos Aires: Editorial Sudamericana, 2013)

Marquez, Nicolás, *La Guerra Civil Argentina. Los 70s que oculta la corrección política* (Buenos Aires: Grupo Unión, 2020)

Martin, Eloy, & Rodriguez, Oscar Luis, *La Aviación en el Ejército Argentino. Crónica Histórica y Catálogo 1867–1991* (Buenos Aires: Talleres Gráficos NH Impresiones, 1991)

Mazzei, Daniel, *Bajo el poder de la Caballería. El Ejército Argentino (1962–1973)* (Buenos Aires: Editorial Eudeba, 2000)

Méndez, Eugenio, *Aramburu: el crimen perfecto* (Buenos Aires: Editorial Sudamericana-Planeta, 1987)

Núñez Padín, Jorge F., *BAC Canberra BMk.62 & TMk.64, Serie Fuerza Aérea #11* (Bahía Blanca: Ediciones Jorge Félix Núñez Padín, 2014)

Núñez Padín, Jorge F., *Dassault Mirage IIICJ/BJ & IIIEA/DA, Serie Fuerza Aérea #23* (Bahía Blanca: Ediciones Jorge Félix Núñez Padín, 2013)

Padín, Jorge F., *McDonnell Douglas A-4P Skyhawk, Serie Fuerza Aérea No. 26* (Bahía Blanca: Ediciones Jorge Félix Núñez Padín, 2016)

Page, Joseph A., *Perón, A biography* (New York: Random House, 1st Edition, 1983)

Pavlovcic, Gabriel, & Raczynski, Esteban, *Helicópteros en la Fuerza Aérea Argentina, Historia y Legado, 1ª Edición Especial* (Buenos Aires: Artes Gráficas del Sur S.R.L., 2022)

Portugheis, Rosa Elsa, *Documentos del Estado Terrorista, Cuadernos del Archivo Nacional de la Memoria Nro. 4, 1ª Edición* (Buenos Aires: Secretaría de Derechos Humanos, Ministerio de Justicia y Derechos Humanos, Presidencia de la Nación, 2012)

Potash, Robert A., *The Army & Politics in Argentina, 1962–1973. From Frondizi's Fall to the Peronist Restoration* (Stanford, California: Stanford University Press, 1996)

Pozzi, Paolo: *Por las sendas argentinas … El PRT-ERP. La guerrilla marxista, 2da. Edición, Colección Bitácora Argentina* (Buenos Aires: Ediciones Imago Mundi, 2004)

Reato, Ceferino, *Masacre en el comedor. La bomba de Montoneros en la Policía Federal. El atentado más sangriento de los 70* (Buenos Aires: Editorial Sudamericana, 2021)

Reato, Ceferino, *Operación Primicia. El ataque de Montoneros que provocó el golpe de 1976* (Buenos Aires: Editorial Sudamericana, 2010)

Reato, Ceferino, *Operación Traviata. ¿Quién mató a Rucci?* (Buenos Aires: Editorial Sudamericana, 2014)

Sequeira, Sebastián, Cal, Carlos, & Catalayub, Cecilia, *Aviación Naval Argentina* (Mendoza: SS & CC Ediciones, 1984)

Sigal Fogliani, Ricardo Jorge, *Blindados Argentinos, de Uruguay y Paraguay* (Buenos Aires: Editorial Ayer y Hoy Ediciones, 1997)

Sprei, Carlos, *La infiltración del Batallón de Inteligencia No. 601 en el PRT-ERP, 1974–1976: el Oso Ranier, ni héroe ni traidor*, 1st Edition (La Plata: Facultad de Humanidades y Ciencias de la Educación, Universidad Nacional de La Plata, 2021) (Digital Book)

Yofre, Juan Bautista, *1976. La conspiración. 24 de marzo. Civiles y Militares en el día que cambió la Argentina* (Buenos Aires: Editorial Sudamericana, 2013)

Yofre, Juan Bautista, *Fuimos todos: Cronología de un fracaso 1976–1983* (Buenos Aires: Editorial Sudamericana, 2014)

Yofre, Juan Bautisra, *Nadie fue (Edición Definitiva). Crónica, documentos y testimonios de los últimos meses, días y horas de Isabel Perón* (Buenos Aires: Editorial Sudamericana, 2011)

University thesis

Larraquy, Marcelo, *La política militar de Montoneros durante el Proceso de Reorganización Nacional (1976–1980). Tesis de Licenciatura en Historia. Facultad de Filosofía y Letras, Universidad de Buenos Aires (UBA)* (Buenos Aires, 2007)

Articles

Bevilacqua, Gilda, 'Del levantamiento al golpe … (y viceversa): el "Operativo Condor Azul"', *V Jornadas de Trabajo sobre Historia Reciente. Eje temático: 5. Sistema político y organizaciones político-militares* (Universidad de Buenos Aires, no date)

Calandra, Contraalmirante (Ret.) Oscar J., 'Una Malversación Histórica', *Boletín del Centro Naval* magazine, Number 808 (May–August 2004, Buenos Aires)

Garaño, Santiago, 'Ensayo del Terrorismo de Estado en Argentina: El Operativo Independencia (Tucumán, 1975–1977)', *Boletín del Instituto de Historia Argentina y Americana Dr. Emilio Ravignani*, Nro. 54 (2021, Universidad de Buenos Aires, Argentina)

Martin, Eloy, 'La primera baja de la Aviación del Ejército en el Operativo Independencia' (Buenos Aires: pdf file, 2022)

Ministerio de Defensa, Presidencia de la Nación, 'Relevamiento y Análisis Documental de los Archivos de las Fuerzas Armadas 1976–1983', 1ra. Edición (Buenos Aires: Ministerio de Defensa, 2015)

Secretaría de Derechos Humanos de la Nación, 'Registro Unificado de víctimas del terrorismo de estado', *Anexo V. Listado de centros cladestinos de detención y otros lugares de reclusión ilegal del terrorismo de estado en la Argentina entre 1974 y 1983* (Pdf document, no date)

Wainfeld, Mario, & Natason, José, 'Montoneros durante el proceso militar', *Todo es Historia*, No. 347 (Buenos Aires, June 1996)

Web pages

Acciones Terroristas de Movimientos Guerrilleros en Argentina. Centro de Graduados del Liceo Naval Militar 'Almirante Guillermo Brown' in https://www.cglnm.com.ar

Air Operations in *Operativo Independencia* in http://aeromilitaria.gacetaeronautica.com/cmp/subversion/pagina3.htm

Argentine Army Aviation in https://loudandclearisnotenought.blogspot.com/p/ejercito-argentino-cuando-el-4.html

Argentine Air Force, Naval Aviation, Army Aviation, Prefectura Naval Aviation and Gendarmeria Aviation data in https://www.amilarg.com.ar/index.html

Guerrilla groups in https://guerraantisubversivaenlaargentina.blogspot.com/

Victims of terrorist organisations in Argentina in https://celtyv.org/ and also in @AFAVITA1.

NOTES

Chapter 1

1 The *Gaucho* is Argentina's cowboy, a country man who normally works on a ranch.
2 Gutman, Daniel, *Tacuara, Historia de la primera guerrilla urbana argentina* (Buenos Aires: Editorial Vergara, 2003).
3 Not to be confused with the Condor Plan of the 1970s, an agreement, supported by the American government, made by the governments of Argentina, Bolivia, Brazil, Chile, Paraguay and Uruguay for the capture and extradition of subversives.
4 Not related to *El Plumerillo* International Airport in Mendoza.
5 '*Uriburu: Siniestra organización antiargentina eligió a Córdoba*', *Diario Córdoba*, 8 March 1971.
6 https://web.archive.org/web/20120424145205/http://marting.stormpages.com/argentinmasa.htm

Chapter 2

1 https://guerraantisubversivaenlaargentina.blogspot.com/
2 https://guerraantisubversivaenlaargentina.blogspot.com/

Chapter 3

1 https://guerraantisubversivaenlaargentina.blogspot.com/
2 Aranda Durañona, *Comodoro* (Ret.) Oscar Luis, *El Vuelo del Cóndor. Fuerza Aérea Argentina. 1912–2012. Cien años protegiendo nuestro cielo* (Buenos Aires: *Dirección de Estudios Históricos de la Fuerza Aérea Argentina*, 2012).
3 Amores Oliver, Eduardo Juan, *Guía de Aeronaves Militares 1912–2006. Fuerza Aérea Argentina* (Buenos Aires: *Dirección de Estudios Históricos. Fuerza Aérea Argentina*, 2007).
4 https://es.wikipedia.org/wiki/Anexo:Titulares_de_la_Armada_Argentina
5 https://www.histarmar.com.ar/Armada%20Argentina/ListGralBuques900a2003.htm
6 Sequeira, Sebastián; Carlos Cal & Catalayub, Cecilia, *Aviación Naval Argentina* (Mendoza: SS & CC Ediciones, 1984).
7 https://es.wikipedia.org/wiki/Anexo:Titulares_del_Ejercito_Argentino
8 https://www.argentina.gob.ar/ejercito
9 Sigal Fogliani, Ricardo Jorge, *Blindados Argentinos, de Uruguay y Paraguay* (Buenos Aires: *Editorial Ayer y Hoy Ediciones*, 1997).
10 Argentine Army Aviation, in https://loudandclearisnotenought.blogspot.com/p/ejercito-argentino-cuando-el-4.html
11 https://loudandclearisnotenought.blogspot.com/p/gendarmeria-nacional-argentina.html
12 https://es.wikipedia.org/wiki/Policia_Federal_Argentina

Chapter 4

1 Burzaco, Ricardo, *Infierno en el Monte Tucumano. Argentina 1973–1976* (Buenos Aires: *Buró Editor S.A.* 2nd Edition, 1997).
2 Burzaco, Ricardo, *Infierno en el Monte Tucumano. Argentina 1973–1976* (Buenos Aires: *Buró Editor S.A.* 2nd Edition, 1997).

Appendices

1 https://www.fuerzas-armadas.mil.ar/GradosMilitares.aspx
2 https://www.fuerzas-armadas.mil.ar/GradosMilitares.aspx
3 https://www.fuerzas-armadas.mil.ar/GradosMilitares.aspx
4 https://www.argentina.gob.ar/prefecturanaval/jerarquias
5 https://www.argentina.gob.ar/jerarquias-de-gendarmeria-nacional
6 https://es.wikipedia.org/wiki/Policia_Federal_Argentina
7 For the ERP see Burzaco, Ricardo, *Infierno en el Monte Tucumano. Argentina 1973–1976* (Buenos Aires: *Buró Editor S.A.* 2nd Edition, 1997). For the *Montoneros* see Díaz Bessone, General de División Ramón Genaro, *Guerra Revolucionaria en la Argentina.* (Buenos Aires: *Editorial Círculo Militar*, 1988).

ABOUT THE AUTHOR

Antonio Luis Sapienza Fracchia was born in Asunción, Paraguay on 14 May 1960. He graduated from the Catholic University of Asunción where he got a B.A. in Clinical Psychology. He also took specialised English courses at Tulane University of New Orleans, Louisiana, and teaching methodology at San Diego State University in California. He is now retired but worked for nearly 40 years as an English Teacher and one of the Academic Coordinators at the Centro Cultural Paraguayo-Americano (CCPA), a bi-national institute in Asunción. Married with two children, he resides in the Capital. He is an Aviation Historian who has written more than 500 articles in specialised magazines and web pages on Paraguayan Aviation History, and has given numerous lectures in schools, universities, institutes and military and civil institutions in Paraguay and abroad. Since 2010, he has been an aviation history professor in the Paraguayan Air Force (FAP). He has published 24 books since 1996, this one being his eleventh with Helion. He has received a total of six decorations for his academic merits, two from Argentina, one from Brazil and three from his own country, Paraguay.